LEARNING TO FISH IN THE TWENTY-FIRST CENTURY

LEARNING TO FISH IN THE TWENTY-FIRST CENTURY

Navigating

the

Career Waters

to

FIND *and* LAND

a

Choice Position

DONNA CHLOPAK, PhD

LEARNING TO FISH IN THE TWENTY-FIRST CENTURY
NAVIGATING THE CAREER WATERS TO FIND
AND LAND A CHOICE POSITION

iUniverse books may be ordered through booksellers or by contacting:

iUniverse
1663 Liberty Drive
Bloomington, IN 47403
www.iuniverse.com
1-800-Authors (1-800-288-4677)

ISBN: 978-1-4917-9443-2 (sc)
ISBN: 978-1-4917-9444-9 (e)

Library of Congress Control Number: 2016907991

Print information available on the last page.

iUniverse rev. date: 5/31/2016

CONTENTS

BACKGROUND

I decided to write this book because I have been teaching a university course in career management / career development during the past several years and have found that many students, college counselors, parents, and others seek guidance in this area. I have a PhD in industrial organizational psychology and more than thirty years of professional business experience, working with all levels of businesses as a manager and consultant. Adding to my knowledge and perspective are my fifteen years of university teaching to both graduate and undergraduate students who are seeking their first step in their careers or a change of job direction. During my teaching, I have developed a process that has benefitted many who are in search of their first position and others who are seeking to obtain a new/different position, including those desiring to change career direction. This book has grown out of these experiences, and I have included many of the exercises that I have my students complete to better connect with a position that is right for them.

It is estimated that most people spend a minimum of eighty-six thousand* hours in jobs during their lifetimes. Considering the number of hours spent at work, those who are connected to their positions are healthier, more effective, and more productive. We spend too much of our lives at work, without getting satisfaction or even enjoyment from what we do for a living. Hopefully, going through this book and some of the exercises will help you find a position that will provide you fulfillment.

Learning to Fish covers the complete process of career management, no matter where you are on your journey or what stage you are at on the path to securing a position.

---

* This was calculated assuming people work from ages twenty-two to sixty-five (or forty-three total years, although many begin work before twenty-two and work into their seventies or eighties). It was based on working eight hours a day (although most people work more), five days a week (although some work six or even seven), for fifty weeks a year. The result is a huge amount of time, and most people in salaried and nonsalaried positions work even more hours, assuming fifty to sixty hours a week. Even if they have more vacation (I assumed two weeks for this estimate), the hours in forty-three years of work will add up to well over one hundred thousand hours of working time.

INTRODUCTION

The title of this book, *Learning to Fish in the Twenty-First Century*, came from the Chinese proverb, "If you give a man a fish, you will feed him for a day. If you teach a man to fish, you will feed him for a lifetime."** I hope that this book will provide some of the knowledge and skills for you to begin to chart your career journey, alter it where needed and desired, and *eat for a lifetime*.

Where are you in your career journey? Ask yourself the following:

- Are you looking for your first professional position?
- Are you in the process of reassessing where you are on your career journey?
- Are you interested in changing jobs? Companies?
- Do you think the grass is greener in another position?
- Do you feel disengaged at your current position? Firm?

If you have answered yes to any of the above questions, then *Learning to Fish* is a guide to help you attract and land that new position. Finding a position with a company that you feel utilizes your talents, abilities, interests, and strengths will provide you with the opportunities to succeed and flourish. Remember the Confucius quote, "Choose a job you love, and you will never have to work a day

---

** This quote has been attributed to many, but I chose to state it was from a Chinese proverb, since an Internet search found this to be the most often referenced source.

in your life." This may be an exaggeration, but it is important to enjoy and feel fulfilled in your work.

The book is arranged in three major sections. The first section (chapters 1 and 2) covers the steps that will help you determine work areas that will bring you enjoyment, fulfillment, and success. You must first understand yourself in terms of what you like to do, situations where you are most comfortable, and what you are good at doing. Knowing yourself will provide you direction in what to look for in a job and company. The second section (chapters 3 and 4) covers the important areas of knowing how to search and network for positions in your areas of interest. While this search is the topic of the second section, this portion of the book also provides direction in understanding what companies are seeking and how to understand if you are a fit or not. Knowing who you are—and identifying potential positions and companies that will be fulfilling, engaging, and a good fit—you will be poised to start the application process. Having reached this point, in the third section of the book (chapters 5 through 8) you will need to create a compelling cover letter and résumé so that the company can decide whether or not to interview you. Preparing for the interview is also included in the third portion of the book, along with what to do when you are offered a position.

CHAPTER 1
KNOWING YOURSELF

Step 1: Autobiography

As you begin to determine your career path—or an alternative route you want to go down—you should start by knowing yourself. Knowing where your talents lie, where you are most comfortable, and what you enjoy doing will help lead you to where you will be happiest and most successful at work. This is an important place to start, since research shows that enjoying your work leads to success. I ask my students to write an autobiography as a first step, as it's a way for them to better understand their foundation for a job search.

In writing your personal story, you can begin by asking yourself some of the following questions:

1. Who is your family?
   a. Where did you grow up? (urban, suburban, rural)
   b. Number of locations? Moves?
   c. Siblings? Birth order?
2. What is your background?
   a. Ethnicity?
   b. Languages spoken?
   c. Family culture and traditions?

3. What activities/hobbies do you enjoy?
   a. Sports played?
   b. Clubs you belong to (e.g., scouting, debate, sororities, etc.)?
   c. Instruments played?
   d. Things collected?
   e. Pets owned?
   f. Hobbies—ways you spend your free time?
   g. Are you a risk taker? Do you enjoy challenges?
4. What are you most proud of having done? (recent and long-term accomplishments, awards, etc.)
   a. What obstacles have you overcome?
   b. What can you do that most others cannot?
5. What are your favorite subject(s)?
6. What is your educational experience? (degrees, certifications, licenses)
7. What jobs have you had?
   a. Paid jobs?
   b. Internships?
   c. Volunteer work?
8. What matters to you in terms of work?
   a. Is your success tied to the amount of money you make?
   b. Are your friends and family more important than career?
   c. What would you be willing to do to get ahead?
   d. What can you contribute to the world through your career?
9. Additional questions to guide your understanding of what type of work you would be happiest doing:
   a. What really makes you happy?
   b. Will your career choice give this to you?
   c. Does your career choice suit your genuine interests?
   d. Does your current career choice really motivate you?
   e. Are you working toward this career for convenience or passion?
   f. Would you rather work inside or outside?
   g. Are you more of a leader or a follower?

h. Do you want to travel with your work?

i. Are you truly grounded in your ethics?

j. What do you want from your career?

In addition to including your behaviors, experiences, education, and tangible activities in your autobiography, you should think about your personal values, wants, dreams, yearnings, and the intangibles of who you are. Table 1 below will also help you to think about yourself and what type of position and company would be the best fit.

Table 1: Thinking about Who You Are

Learning/Education, Mental Abilities	Morals, Values	Culture, Family
What I know and have learned: degrees, certifications, licenses, talents, skills, experiences, common sense, problem solving, critical thinking,	What defines my character: ethics, choices and decisions reactions principles values pressure time commitment	Background, Family Culture, ethnicity, language heritage, norms, traditions national original
Wants, desires	**Outward – what others see**	**Inward – my feelings**
What do I want? dreams What are my goals? immediate, stretch future direction, getting there	My health, appearance, body type habits –healthy vs. nonhealthy age statue resulting impression	What drives me – heart or head emotional intelligence -self knowledge emotional intelligence-reading others strengths interests biggest obstacles

Beliefs, Principles	Relationships	Economic Drivers
What I believe my religion focus on self focus on others	Social, work, volunteer friendships vs. acquaintances introvert vs. extrovert reserved outgoing confident risk-taking	Where I am, where I want to be needs vs. wants realistic expectations

After reviewing table 1 and responding to the items, answering the questions in table 2 below will help you define who you are, so that you can better focus on companies and positions that are a good fit for you.

Table 2: Thinking about What You Like and Want

Questions	Your Responses
What activities do you enjoy?	
1. Do you like to work with people?	
2. Do you like to work with numbers?	
3. Do you prefer to work with ideas?	
4. Do you prefer to work with processes and procedures?	
5. Are you a risk taker? Do you enjoy challenges?	
6. What are your favorite subject(s)?	
7. What matters most to you in terms of work?	
8. Is your success tied to the amount of money you make?	
9. Are your friends and family more important than career?	
10. What would you be willing to do to get ahead?	
11. What do you hope to contribute to the world through your career?	

Questions	Your Responses
12. Is your success tied to the amount of money you make?	
13. Are your friends and family more important than career?	
14. What do you hope to contribute to the world through you career?	
Additional questions to guide your understanding of what type of work you would be happiest doing:	
15. What really makes you happy?	
16. Will your career choice give this to you?	
17. Does your career choice suit your genuine interests/passions?	
18. Does your current career choice really motivate you?	
19. Are you working toward this career for convenience or passion?	
20. Would you rather work inside or outside?	
21. Are you more of a leader or a follower?	
22. Do you want to travel with your work?	
23. Are you truly grounded in your ethics?	
24. What do you want from your career?	

Step 2: Personal Assessments

In addition to writing your autobiography and answering the previous questions, there are a number of professionally designed assessments that can add to your self-understanding. These assessments have been developed with scoring mechanisms that provide data in comparison to other individuals, so that you can measure your strengths, interests, skills, and personality types to provide additional information for your understanding of *you*.

You can find many different types of assessments by going on the Internet and entering any of the following key words: occupational assessments, interest inventories, strengths assessments, personality tests, and the like. Appendix A has several links to free assessments. Remember that the value of the assessment is often in its interpretation, and those that come with no cost also usually have no individual consulting. Most of the sites do provide additional learning to help you get the most from your results, and I advise you to utilize their additional learning or exercises.

I will focus on two different types of assessments below: a *strengths* assessment and an *interest* assessment. The strengths assessment measures the unique and enduring ways that you engage in a role, while the interest assessment provides you with information on your interests and drives.

Strengths: Although the Gallup Organization developed the original Clifton *StrengthsFinder* assessment,[1] several other organizations have since developed similar assessments. Strengths are defined as the unique and enduring ways that you do what you do and that primarily drive you instinctively. WorkUno has a similar assessment of strengths that is free and can be accessed through the following link: http://freestrengthstest.workuno.com/free-strengths-test.html.

The WorkUno assessment asks you to rate your agreement using a nine-point scale on 170 items. This is not a forced-choice assessment, so the results can be overlapping, and your list of strengths can all be high, low, or in a range.

In addition to being free, another benefit of this link is that it provides you with a complete list of your strengths from one to thirty-four. When you get your complete list of your thirty-four strengths, consider the top five to ten areas that you feel most reflect your strengths. You should focus on your top five to ten strengths, (depending on the intensity of the rating, i.e., how high is the number associated with your individual rating), and the bottom five to determine your *nonstrengths*. To really know yourself, it is important to know what both your strengths and nonstrengths are. I suggest that you go to the link and take the assessment. When you have taken the assessment, you can return here and continue once you have your results.

Table 3 lists the thirty-four strength themes that define the way one works. Strengths do not point you to a particular field of work or an industry, but knowing your strengths can help you to better understand the way you work and can help direct you to the type of work that fits you best and would be enjoyable.

Table 3: Thirty-Four Strength Themes

achiever	activator	adaptability	analytical	arranger
belief	command	communication	competition	connectedness
consistency	context	deliberative	developer	discipline
empathy	focus	futuristic	harmony	ideation
includer	individualization	input	intellection	learner
maximizer	positivity	relator	responsibility	restorative
	self assurance	significance	strategic	WOO (winning others over)

Knowing your strengths will allow you to focus on what you do best. For example, if you have competition as a top theme, knowing the specific goals or outcomes of your job (e.g., having a goal of selling fifteen cars in a month or working in a job where employees are ranked against each other for bonuses) will fit your top strength. Whereas, if harmony is one of your top themes, you would be more comfortable working in a team where there is a consensus on methods and goals.

The strengths have been grouped into four theme areas—relating, impacting, striving, and thinking, as described below:

1. Relating themes: communication, empathy, harmony, includer, individualization, relator, responsibility.
2. Impacting themes: command, competition, developer, maximizer, positivity, WOO.
3. Striving themes: achiever, activator, adaptability, belief, discipline, focus, restorative, self-assurance, significance.
4. Thinking themes: analytical, arranger, connectedness, consistency, context, deliberative, futuristic, ideation, input, intellection, learner, strategic.

Your top strengths may fall in all four areas or focused in just one or two. This will also help you find the direction of the types of positions that will be your best fit and how you work. For example, if most of your strengths are in the relating and impacting themes, then you will want to look for positions that are highly involved with people—like customer service or management. If most of your strengths are in the thinking themes area, then you are more likely to want a position that allows you to learn and analyze, such as a market research or business analyst.

You can find more information about the thirty-four strengths and their specific definitions at http://www.workuno.com or http://www.gallup.com/home.aspx sites and in appendix B.

Once you have completed your strengths assessment, it is helpful to ask yourself some questions to delve into your results and use what you discover. These questions will help you to better understand how to use the assessment in your career efforts and also help you identify partners and people to work with who have complementary strengths. *Note:* it is helpful to find partners with complementary strengths, so that your area of *nontalent* will not hold you back. Partnering with someone who can "fill in the gaps" will take some of the burden off you and help you both succeed. (These questions are also found in appendix C with space for writing your answers.)

1. What strengths are at the top of your results? What were at the bottom? Were they what you expected? Did anything surprise you?

2. How have you seen your strengths play a role in your life— both personally and at work? How have the nonstrengths impacted you?

3. If you could do any job, what would it be? What makes it appealing? How do you think it fits with your strengths?

4. Are you prepared to do that job right now? If yes, is there anything holding you back? If no, what is holding you back? How do your strengths or nonstrengths help or hinder your preparedness?

5. Do you have a view of where you would like to be in three to five years? What steps do you think will help you get there? What opportunities would support your journey? What might be obstacles? How can you use your strengths to assist in this effort?

6. Of the positions you have held, what has been the most rewarding? What has been the most disappointing? If you view these from the perspective of your strengths, can you learn anything that will help you in the future?

Consider your top five to ten strengths as those areas that you lead with in terms of how you are most comfortable approaching tasks.

What ways do you best handle situations, problems, requests, hobbies, work situations, or leisure activities? Think of the bottom five as areas that you will need to manage around or find a complementary partner/coworker to help you with, as these areas are nontalents that you will often struggle with and are unlikely to excel in.

Once you feel you have an understanding of your strengths and any other personality or behavioral assessment information, it is helpful to see where your interests lie.

[1]*Note:* The Gallup Organization developed the original Clifton StrengthsFinder assessment (more detailed information can be found in *Now Discover Your Strengths* or *Strengths 2.0* in bookstores or online at the Gallup site). That assessment consists of a number of paired-comparison statements in which you indicate how close you are to one or the other statement. This forced-choice assessment results in an ordered list of strengths by weight, based on your ratings. You can take the Gallup StrengthsFinder assessment if you purchase one of their books, as they usually come with a code to access their online assessment. However, the results are only a list of your top five strengths. This is useful, but the books will help you delve more deeply into their theory and philosophy.

Interests: Your interests will also inform your career choice and should be assessed. There are several interest inventories available on the Internet. Two free assessments are from Career Outlook and Career Thesaurus. Career Outlook's interest profile can be found at careeroutlook.us/assessment/short.shtml. This assessment has you rate your level of interest on a three-point scale (Like, Unsure, Dislike) on sixty items. The results of your assessment are defined in six areas according to those items you like. See table 4 to see the result categories and their definitions. This site also provides recommendations based on your scores.

Table 4: Career Outlook Assessment Outcome Categories

Interest Areas	Definitions
realistic	Doers
enterprising	Persuaders
investigative	Thinkers
artistic	Creators
social	Helpers
conventional organizers	Routine/set procedures

www.careerthesaurus.com has an assessment that consists of three steps. The first step is a forced choice on nine items, listed below in table 5.

Table 5: Choice Options of the Career Thesaurus Assessment

Option A	Option B
working in a social setting	working alone
working outside	working at a desk
concerned with processes	concerned with results
focused	relaxed
concerned with data/facts	concerned with imagination/intuition
rational	emotional
work in office	work remotely
like established processes	like discovery
want fixed compensation	willing to have variable compensation

Step 2 is to choose as many of the twenty-one potential areas of interest (listed in table 6).

Table 6: Career Thesaurus Potential Areas of Interest

competitiveness	scientific method/ perfection	machinery
helping others	beauty/visual perfection	working with people
risk aversion	being in the spotlight	body strength
safety of others	nature and animals	coordinating groups
hand labor	politics and strategy	drafting and sketching
sense of duty	technology and gadgets	giving critical advice
creativity	working with numbers	sales

Finally, you are asked your level of education, and the immediate results are given to you as three potential jobs of interest. You are also able to go back as many times as you wish to alter your responses. This is a fun and quick assessment, but the results are more general than those of other assessments.

The two assessments discussed are free and more limited than the Career Occupational Preference System (COPS) I use in my classes, but you may not have access to the COPS. The interest areas measured by the COPS can be found in table 7 below:

Table 7: COPS Interest Areas

science—medical life	business—finance
science—physical	business—management
technology—electrical	communication—written
technology—mechanical	communication—oral
technology—civil	arts—performing
outdoor—nature	arts—design
outdoor—agribusiness	service—instructional
computation	service—social

I have included more information on COPS in appendix D.

Taking an interest inventory can help you focus your efforts in career areas that fit with what you usually do best. Strengths are generic in that they can be applied to all areas of work. Interests, however, will direct you to certain industries or disciplines. If we go back to the fishing analogy, strengths will point you to the type of equipment you are most comfortable using in your quest for your dinner, but interests will help determine your target catch—be it tuna, salmon, or trout.

Step 3: Summary of You

Having completed your autobiography, done your strengths assessment, and identified and completed at least one interest inventory, you should have a pretty good picture of who *you* are.

Knowing where you want to go—knowing your goal—will help you determine the steps you need to get there. Previous work and school experiences will also guide you to areas of interest as you embark on your job search. What have you done in the past that you enjoyed (that didn't seem like *work*—the four letter word), or what have you done in the past that you couldn't finish or get away from quickly enough? Not everyone enjoys working with children, senior citizens, numbers, or physical labor. When you better understand what you enjoy doing, you will find something that both engages you and provides opportunity for career growth. You are now ready to decide in what career waters you should be fishing.

CHAPTER 2
WHAT DO YOU WANT TO DO?
(NARROWING YOUR SEARCH)

Most full-time working people spend a minimum of two thousand hours a year at their jobs. That is probably more time than you spend on any other single activity in your year. A standard workday is eight hours—a third of your day—and most of us work more than an eight-hour day. Add to that the time it takes to get to and from work, time to get ready in the morning, and any time outside of the office that you spend thinking about or doing work—and you see that it takes up the bulk of your waking hours. The graph below shows a daily breakdown of activities on average for working people on weekdays.

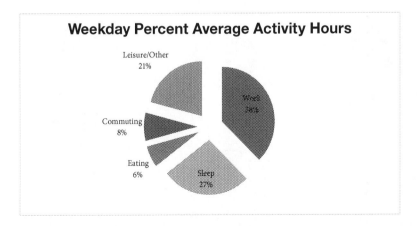

Weekday Percent Average Activity Hours

Leisure/Other 21%

Commuting 8%

Eating 6%

Work 38%

Sleep 27%

Given that you will be spending so many hours at your job, it is important for both your health and the health of the organization that you enjoy—or at least do not hate—your job. There are several decisions to consider as you go about your job search, and it's best to think of these when you begin to lay out your career plan. Keeping in mind *you*—who you are and where you want to be (i.e., your goals)—narrow down the type of position and the type of company you are interested in working for. The next two discussions will help you to focus. They will enable you to more fully understand actual jobs and organizational cultures, so you can narrow your search and help ensure that your final catch will be a fit based on both the work itself and the organization.

Section 1: Work Environment

In addition to the position itself and the work you will be doing, the culture or work environment plays a key role in your fit at an organization. Environment at work encompasses several areas: location, office space/setup, company size, company culture, mobility, and so forth. Some of these areas may have been uncovered in your previous assessment of interests.

- Do you want to work in an office at a desk, or do you want to work in offices but go from place to place (e.g., traveling between clients or company facilities)? Or do you want at least some of your time to be spent working outdoors?
- Do you want to work in a large company where you might only interact with your department? Or do you want to work in a small company where you are more likely to know and work with everyone in the firm?
- Do you want to work in a start-up where it is likely that their policies and procedures are still developing? Or do you want to work in an established firm with solid processes in place?
- Do you want to work in a company that values innovation and entrepreneurship? Or do you prefer a staid/established firm with set rituals, rules, and procedures?
- Do you want to work in an organization with flexible schedules and be able to work remotely? Or would you prefer more of a nine-to-five expected schedule where you are in the office?
- Do you want to work with your hands or mainly with your brain? All positions require an *engaged brain*, but not all jobs require physical exertion or manual labor.
- Do you want to work in a company that offers training and advancement? Or are you more interested in having more leisure time?

- Are you interested in working overseas for a firm that moves workers around often? Or are you locked into your current geography?

These areas of question (type of work, work environment, and organization culture) will help you to determine a position that best fits you and the type of firm you would most like to work for. Once you have answered the above questions, you will be able to move to the next section. The answers to these questions will help determine and focus your search.

To enhance your search efforts, you will need to begin doing informational interviews. Informational interviews are just that—seeking to get additional information about a position/job and a company to determine the fit.

Section 2: Informational Interviews: Learning about a Position/Job

It is important for you to fully understand what a position entails and what a company expects from you before accepting a position. If you know someone in the type of position you are seeking, have an honest conversation with him or her regarding what the job is really all about. Questions might include: How much time do they spend in various activities? What do they like most about it? Least about it? In table 8 (and also in appendix E), there is a list of beginning questions to ask regarding the position. These types of interviews are necessary to make sure that you have a good idea what the work is and what is required of someone in the position.

If you don't really know the person, ask for ten to fifteen minutes of his or her time for an initial interview. Depending on how that goes, you can seek further information from additional contacts. If you do not know anyone in the specific type of position, then network with friends, relatives, faculty, and acquaintances to see if they can suggest someone in the desired position who they can introduce you to.

Table 8: Questions That Define Positions

1. What does a typical day look like in this position?
2. What do you like most about this job?
3. What do you like least about this job?
4. What most surprises you about this position?
5. What would you like to change about this position?
6. What background (education and experience) did you need to get this position?
7. What did you do right before you began this job?
8. What do you wish you had known before taking this job that you know now?
9. What do you wish you could do more of at this job?
10. What do you wish there was less of at this job?
11. If you had to do it over again, what other classes and/or work experiences would you have taken/gotten before starting this job?
12. If you could have any job, what would it be and why (if not this one)?

Many people have faulty expectations about a position, based on books they've read, television depictions, or casual conversations with people in the job. As is often said, "the grass is always greener on the other side of the fence." However, without really having an accurate picture of the position's expectations, you could think you are getting your dream position only to find out it is more of a nightmare—or at least not a fit with your original beliefs. Without accurate information about the company, the job, and expectations for the position, you will not be fully equipped to make an informed job decision. It is somewhat like seeing someone across a room at a party, and you are instantly attracted to them due to their looks. But when you go to meet the person, you find that he or she doesn't meet your expectations. The person is too young / too old, too smart / not smart enough, too deep / too shallow, has an unpleasant voice, or doesn't match your expectations in some other way.

Keep in mind that more than one of these interviews is helpful, as people in the same position often have somewhat different perspectives of the job. It is also good to interview position holders from different firms, as expectations might vary depending on the company. Large and small companies differ greatly, public and private firms differ, and industries differ in their expectations of similar positions. For example, a position in human resources in a small company probably encompasses recruiting, hiring, compensation, performance evaluation, benefits administration, development and training, succession planning, and firing. However, a human resources position in a large company could be focused only on training and development.

An example of why this is important is a situation that occurred in my class. A student wanted to be an entrepreneur and own his own landscaping firm. He found a landscaping business owner and interviewed him about his business and what his job entailed. The student found out that the business owner spent one week a month doing paperwork about billing and collections. The student decided at that point that he no longer wanted this job.

Informational interviews about positions can provide you with a clearer understanding of job expectations. This will help you choose wisely in your job focus and help your commitment once you're hired. For example, you interviewed a car salesman in a dealership that you knew closed at six on Saturday evening, and you were surprised to find out that he was often tied up finalizing a sale with a customer until nine thirty or ten on Saturday nights. Therefore, you might have decided that this wasn't a fit for you, as you have a standing appointment at eight in the evening on Saturdays.

Research has shown that realistic job previews support both employee success and therefore improved company performance. This is because a realistic job preview lets applicants know what they are committing to and to begin their jobs with their eyes wide open. It is important to understand the expectations of a position you're considering, so that you can be prepared and know what you are committing to.

Another benefit to doing informational interviews is the insight and additional knowledge you gain about the position, if and when you are asked for an interview. In chapter 7 on interviewing, you will see how this background can serve to bolster your interview performance.

Section 3: Informational Interviews: Learning about the Company/Work Environment

In addition to understanding what is expected in a job, it is helpful to understand the company's work environment and culture. You can get help choosing a specific company by going to job fairs, speaking to friends and relatives, or just checking out company websites. Your answers in section 1 can also provide guidance in your selection process.

As stated above, since you will be spending at least a third of your weekdays in this company, it is important to be comfortable in the company culture. You can gather information about a company by looking through its website or seeing if there is data about the company on the web (e.g., www.GlassDoor.com, www.GreatPlacestoWork). Again, doing your own research with an informational interview will help you make better decisions about your fit with a company and how it operates. You can interview someone you already know, network to obtain a contact who works in the company, or call human resources to ask for assistance. In speaking to someone who actually works in the company, you will get firsthand knowledge of how the policies are carried out rather than just what is written in the company handbook.

LinkedIn™ is also a potential source for identifying someone in a company who may be able to provide information. Table 9 (and appendix F) has a beginning list of potential questions to ask someone who is working in the firm about the company's culture and way of doing things. Your questions should be driven by what is important to you and what will help you make a good decision about a potential employer.

Table 9: Questions That Define Company/Work Environments

1.	What do you like most about working for this company?
2.	What do you dislike most about working for this company?
3.	Do you feel recognized for your accomplishments at this firm?
4.	How would you rate the management at the company?
5.	Do you feel that there is opportunity for advancement at this company? If yes, what does it take to advance?
6.	Would you state that this company is focused on production or people or both? Why?
7.	What has been your biggest surprise since joining this company?
8.	If you could change anything about this company, what would it be?
9.	Is there anything that you hope never changes about the company?
10.	If you could work for any company, which one would you choose and why?

A Fishing Analogy: You are interested in fishing for salmon for dinner (landing a job). Scenario 1: You have the wrong equipment (i.e., you don't know what the job really entails). You have a rod and reel but it is lightweight and cannot hold a forty-five-pound salmon. Even if you managed to hook a salmon (get an interview), your line and rod could break (they would not offer you the job after the interview). Scenario 2: You had all the right equipment, and you are successful in getting your forty-five-pound salmon into the boat (you got called for the interview, aced it, and were offered the job), but you find out that the waters you fished in were polluted. You can't eat that salmon for dinner (you couldn't/shouldn't accept the offer). That would be like landing what appeared to be a great job but in a company that had a culture that wasn't a fit.

Once you have done your informational interviews and are comfortable that you have a direction in terms of type of work/

position and company, you are ready to continue on a focused job search. You can continue your informational interviews throughout your job search, as such efforts provide valuable data about a prospective position and company. As you progress in your career journey, these interviews become part of your normal course of networking and meeting new people.

CHAPTER 3
LOOKING FOR WORK
(AND BEING FOUND)

Based on your understanding of your strengths, talents, experiences, and interests, you should have a pretty good idea of the kind of position you are seeking and the type of company that is a good fit for you. Therefore, you are ready to start your search.

In today's Internet world, there are new opportunities for accessing your job hunt through the World Wide Web. However, looking for work on the web has both benefits and liabilities. There are many job sites where you can set up an ongoing search that will send potential job openings to your e-mail on a regular basis. Some of these sites allow you to specify certain search criteria to narrow down what opportunities you receive. Some examples of the criteria include the following: type of position, educational background, years of experience, compensation requirements, and so on. Note that not all sites are as specific as you may want, and you may be sent job openings that aren't really a good fit for you. In addition, you can go directly to company websites to seek out openings in the firm.

I have listed the most popular general sites in table 10, and table 11 provides a short list of sites focused on students, internships, and entry-level positions. You can find additional job sites that aren't used as much in appendix G.

These sites are often free, so there is also a benefit there. The potential downside of these sites is that not all jobs are listed on them, and they aren't always updated when the positions are filled. In addition, your search criteria might be limited to their screening mechanisms, which might not be as specific as you would like. So you may be sent a lot of sales jobs in both pharmaceutical and payroll businesses, but perhaps you have no experience or interest in the drug companies—so only some of the positions are a good fit.

Table 10: General Job Sites

Site	Description
http://www.careerbuilder.com	CareerBuilder provides listings and résumé postings for both local and national jobs.
http://www.dice.com	Dice is a site for tech job seekers. It allows searching by company, job title, location, and key word.
http://www.Glassdoor.com	Glassdoor is a site that helps both job seekers and companies connect. The site provides user-generated content regarding salary reports, individual candidate and employee ratings, and reviews.
http://INDEED.com	Indeed aggregates job listings from various websites, including company career pages, job boards, newspaper classifieds, associations, and other online sources of job postings.
http://Ladders.com	The Ladders site is for more experienced job seekers, as it focuses on six-figure positions and higher.

Site	Description
http://LinkedIn.com	LinkedIn connects professionals and provides opportunities to connect and network on the Internet.
http://LinkUp.com	LinkUp monitors thousands of company career websites and provides listings that are often unadvertised elsewhere.
http://Monster.com	Monster, which is one of the original job listings, includes the ability to search for positions and post résumés.
http://SimplyHired.com	Search engines on SimplyHired connect job seekers and employers.
http://TweetMyJobs.com	TweetMyJobs is a global social and mobile recruiting platform. The site provides jobs to Twitter through job channels that are segmented by geography, job type, and industry to connect employers and seekers.
http://USJobs.com	National Labor Exchange's website is derived from a partnership between the Direct Employers Association and the National Association of State Workforce Agencies (NASWA). It is designed to directly connect employers, recruiters, and job seekers.

Table 11: Job Sites for Students (Internships and Entry-Level Positions)

Site	Description
http://CollegeTopTalent.com	CollegeTopTalent.com is dedicated to helping college students and recent grads find entry-level jobs and internships. It allows you to create a profile, résumé, and even a video.

Site	Description
http://YouTern.com	YouTern.com connects talent to high-impact internships and mentors through its community that provides support for college students, recent graduates, young professionals, career center pros, and all-star career experts.
http://Internships.com	Internships.com brings students, employers, and higher education institutions together in one centralized location. The site provides a wide variety of interactive tools and services to connect students to internship opportunities.
http://CareerRookie.com	CareerRookie.com's focus is on students and recent graduates seeking internships, part-time jobs, and entry-level positions and connecting them with employers. CareerRookie.com is a division of CareerBuilder.
http://CollegeRecruiter.com	CollegeRecruiter.com is a niche job site for college students searching for internships and recent graduates hunting for entry-level jobs and other career opportunities. It has won WEDDLE's Award for Best Job Boards six years in a row.

Looking on individual company websites for openings is also a possibility, since many companies list their openings. Some even have a place to register for future positions that fit your criteria. The traditional means of job searching are also still available—newspapers, professional publications, and networking with friends and relatives. An executive search firm or headhunter's efforts are also a possibility for higher-level positions, and these often specialize in industries or unique positions.

Section 1: Being Found

The web also provides you with a presence that employers can access, so you should be cautious about what you post on your social media sites or blog about. Even what your personal e-mail address handle  is can make you end up in the not-considered group (For example, e-mail addresses like HotMama23@gmail.com or TattooGuy45@ yahoo.com send a very wrong message to a potential hiring manager.)

I have heard of a situation where someone posted that they were happy about getting a job and then were informed by the company that the job offer was being retracted, as the company didn't publicize their hires on social media. This is an extreme case, but you can understand if your Facebook page shows you being drunk at a party (i.e., therefore pictured in a less than professional or flattering situation) and a future employer sees the post, they may decide that they do not want such a person representing them.

Keep in mind that the downside of the Internet world is that you have an online presence, and companies can find out about you by what you post and have posted. It may be too late to warn you about putting up that picture of your latest Halloween costume or tattoo on Facebook, but keep in mind that future employers might see something you thought only those on the beach could see. What you post in terms of pictures and words are open to viewing by many—even though you might have thought these images or posts were protected. It's better to be safe than sorry, so beware of your online presence.

Section 2: Your Search—Cautions

During your search, whether you are looking at websites, newspapers, postings on bulletin boards, getting e-mails, or getting notifications from various search engines, it is very important to read the position listing carefully. Be cautious, because if it sounds too good to be true, it probably is. Unfortunately, many recent graduates are seduced by claims for quick advancement, flexible hours, and high pay. Remember the acronym often mentioned in finance classes: TINSTAAFL—pronounced *Tin Staffle*. It stands for "there is no such thing as a free lunch."

Another term for compensation is *earnings*, and you need to actually work for what you are paid. You are embarking on a lifetime journey, and you cannot start at the top or even in the middle without experience, so be cautious and do your research. There are several good sites where you can check out companies of interest. Two are (1) www.Glassdoor.com (as mentioned above) and (2) www.RipOffReport. com. Glassdoor.com covers various types of companies, including Fortune 500s, and often provides information on what is asked in an interview and salary offerings. Ripoffreport.com covers smaller, entrepreneurial firms and has responses from people willing to provide feedback on their experiences with the company.

Remember when you read these reviews that those responding are people who are often disenchanted with the firm and therefore are taking out their frustrations by rating the company on the Internet. However, if there are twenty comments about the company and two are positive and eighteen are negative, that might suggest caution in pursuing a position with that company.

Remember if it looks like a duck, waddles like a duck, and quacks—it probably is a duck.

CHAPTER 4
POSITION ADVERTISEMENTS

Once you think you have found a good potential opportunity, a job ad, the next step is to make sure it is a fit that's worth applying for. It's important to know the steps to put your best self forward to increase your chances of being considered. The following sections will help you determine (1) if it is a good match and (2) how to best position yourself for success.

Section 1: Careful Reading of a Job Ad / Position Description: Are You a Match?

When you find a position of interest, it is imperative that you fully understand what is being sought in a candidate. The job listing might seem straightforward, but there also might be some hints to areas that could boost your opportunity when applying. Most job listings have several parts:

1. An introduction to the company and what they do
2. A summary paragraph about what the job entails
3. A list of job requirements
4. A list of desired skills, certifications, and abilities
5. Company benefits

Reading a job ad/listing carefully can save both you and the recruiter / hiring manager time, as you can eliminate positions that you are not a good fit for, due to any of the areas listed previously. For example, any of the reasons below should deter you from applying, as they would be deficiencies in your application/fit for the position:

1. The position is located in Texas, and you cannot move from New York.
2. The job requires a bilingual person with proficiency in English and German, but you speak English and Spanish.
3. The job requires a Series 7 license, and you don't know what that is, don't have one, or have no interest in pursuing one.
4. The job requires customer service experience, and you don't like working with customers.

Exhibit 1 shows an example of a list of job qualifications that appeared in a job ad for a human resources manager and a copy of the ad highlighted for key areas of focus for a responding cover letter and résumé.

Exhibit 1: Job Ad for Human Resources Manager

Qualifications

- Bilingual English/Spanish necessary.
- Bachelor's degree in human resource management, public administration, business, or closely related field and three to five years of HR-related experience, or seven years of progressively responsible HR-related experience, or equivalent combination of experience and training.
- Plant manufacturing / union avoidance experience preferred. Considerable knowledge of principles and practices of personnel administration.
- Exceptional oral and written communication skills. Good judgment and strong problem resolution skills.
- Excellent organizational and interpersonal skills and the ability to work effectively at all levels of the organization and across other functional areas.
- Ability to maintain a high level of confidentiality. Strong Word, Excel, PowerPoint, and Outlook skills (knowledge of ADP Enterprise, E-Time a definite plus).
- Ability to successfully manage multiple work priorities in a fast-paced environment.

On the next page (exhibit 2) are some highlighted (italics, bold) points that should be addressed in both the cover letter and résumé.

Exhibit 2: Job Ad Focus on Requirements and Items Preferred

Qualifications

- ***Bilingual*** English/Spanish necessary
- ***Bachelor's degree*** in human resource management, public administration, business, or closely related field and ***three to five years of HR-related experience***, or seven years of progressively responsible HR-related experience, or equivalent combination of ***experience and training.***
- *Plant manufacturing / union avoidance experience preferred.* Considerable knowledge of principles and practices of personnel administration.
- ***Exceptional oral and written communication skills. Good judgment and strong problem resolution skills.***
- Excellent organizational and interpersonal skills and the ability to work effectively at all levels of the organization and across other functional areas.
- Ability to maintain a high level of confidentiality. ***Strong Word, Excel, PowerPoint, and Outlook skills*** *(knowledge of ADP Enterprise, E-Time a definite plus).*
- Ability to successfully manage multiple work priorities in a fast-paced environment.

The items that are in italics and bolded are requirements and should be addressed directly with clear and quantitative examples of these behaviors. Items in italics only sections are preferences, and those who can demonstrate that knowledge will have a leg up on the position. The other items listed are somewhat universally listed in most job ads and should be addressed with specific examples wherever possible.

Section 2: Red Flags

What would you do if you saw these in a job ad?

CRM MIS HTML SPSS

Another area of potential caution in a job ad would be the use of acronyms or a list of initials that you don't know the meaning of. For example, if the job ad mentions CRM and you are not familiar with what that series of letters refers to, it might *not* be a good fit for you. However, you can do an Internet search of those three letters, and you might find that you do know what they mean—customer relationship management. You realize that you have even studied that topic in both your marketing and computer science classes, so you might know what they are asking about—and you might be a fit.

Job ads that list requirements that are quite a bit below your experiences (e.g., you have graduated with a bachelor's degree in business administration and they require only a high school diploma) probably aren't worth your time in applying. This is because the hiring manager might label you as overqualified, desperate, unfocused and/or overpriced—and then will pass you by. Also, if you were to get the interview and potentially the job, would that job stimulate you and be a good fit?

Although you may feel that applying for a position that doesn't fit may just be a waste of your time and no real harm, there is another potential downside. Consider if a recruiter / hiring manager remembers your nonfitting / inappropriate application. He or she might subsequently not consider you for a position in the future where you might be a good candidate, particularly if the hiring manager felt that your initial application showed inappropriate focus or lack of attention to detail. So be cautious in your applications; do not waste your time or a recruiter's / hiring manager's time. You don't want your efforts to be a random roll of the dice but rather a focused effort that will be more likely to land you a job that fits and will provide you with an opportunity to begin or continue on your chosen career path.

Section 3: Requirements

When a position listing has requirements, that is just what they are—and you must be able to fulfill them. If there is an *or* listed, make sure that you can demonstrate either of the requirements completely. Often an *or* requires greater explanation, and it is good to make sure that you address it in your cover letter. Education and experience are sometimes listed as interchangeable in a requirements section. If a specific degree is required and you have a degree in another area—but have significant course work and/or experience in the required area—you may be able to explain that in a cover letter also. It is key that you do *not* waste your time or the recruiter's time if you *do not* have what is required for the position. Keep in mind, often there are hundreds of applicants for each opening and recruiters / hiring managers may be annoyed if they feel that their time is being wasted. In the job ad in exhibit 2 the requirements are bolded and in italics.

Section 4: Preferred—Nice to Have

Most position descriptions have a list of skills that they would like you to have (these are in *italics* in exhibit 2). The greater number of these skills that you can *demonstrate* through your cover letter and résumé, the more likely you will be in the employer's short list and possibly be asked for an interview. It is also critical that you actually have these skills and can show examples where you have displayed them, rather than just state that you have them. I often write "fluff" on students' papers when they write that they are "an excellent *comunicater*"—and as you can see, they spelled *communicator* incorrectly, negating their claim.

Additional Examples:

Fluff	Demonstrating Performance
I have strong leadership skills.	I started a club on campus in my freshman year that grew to a membership of 300 students by the senior year, and I served as its president all four years.
I am an experienced salesperson.	I was named leading salesman for 7 out of 12 quarters working in sales for XYZ company.
I am versed in customer satisfaction.	I developed a training program for retail personnel that increased the store's customer satisfaction ratings by 20 percent.

CHAPTER 5
COVER LETTERS

Section 1: Salutation—Personalization

You have now found a position for which you wish to apply, and you are preparing your cover letter. The first step in any letter is the greeting, and you have a chance to stand out if you personalize the salutation. Often a job ad does not specifically list the person to whom you are responding. If this is the case, it is useful to try to find out who will be the recipient of your application. A little extra time spent trying to find out the name of the person will go a long way when you send your letter, as yours might be the only letter that was personally addressed. Making an error in the salutation can also derail your entire application. Below are some *errors* to avoid:

- Dear Mr. Sally Jones, (Sally is not a Mr.)
- Hey, (very unprofessional)
- Sally Jones, (it is better to have a greeting word in addition to the name)
- Sally, (too personal if you don't have a last name and Ms. or Mrs.)
- To whom it may concern, (Recruiter might respond, "It doesn't concern me.")

In today's Internet world, often you are sending something by e-mail, and you might only have a first name in the job listing. If this is the case and you cannot find out to whom the application is going—or anytime when you don't know the name of the person to whom you are sending the letter—it is okay to use the job title as an option rather than having no salutation. For example, you could write, Dear Hiring Manager, or Dear Recruiting Manager, or Dear (title of who the position is reporting to), or any title that might be mentioned as receiving these applications.

Section 2: Introduction

You begin the cover letter with a statement of the position you are applying for and where you heard about it. This provides the hiring manager some background and helps them focus on your information, as they may be looking at candidates for several positions at the same time. Also, by stating where you heard about the opening, they will have some insight into you and their recruiting practices. If you found the job on their website versus hearing about it on Career Builder, they know you are interested in their company in particular. Sometimes different job ad placements differ slightly, and that would also help them in determining your fit. You are responding to a specific ad, and they can see how you fit what was listed as required and desired. There is no need to introduce yourself by name in the first line of the letter or to state your name, as the reader will have it at the end of the letter and it will seem awkward and a waste of space. Exhibit 3 shows some examples.

Exhibit 3: Examples of Cover Letter Introductions

Poor Introduction	I found your ad for an internship and know that I am a perfect fit for it.

Poor Introduction	I read of your job and am excited about the opportunity of working for your firm.
Good Introduction	I read of your opening for a junior business analyst in Los Angeles on the Bank of America website and am excited about the possibility of joining your company in this capacity.
Good Introduction	I found your job ad for a marketing manager in your pet food division on Indeed.com and am interested in the position.

Section 3: Fit for the Position

Once you state what position you are seeking, it is important to state why you are a fit for this position. Make sure that you address the requirements stated in the ad and, where possible, how you meet the desired skills. Make it compelling by listing your accomplishments that fit the position and support your claim of being the "ideal candidate." It is important to dimension your accomplishments with numbers. Don't just state vague information about improving productivity, increasing efficiency, growing sales, or reducing shrink; instead, make sure that you put numbers to these statements and quantify your successes. Exhibit 4 shows some examples of weak and strong statements.

Exhibit 4: Ways to Strengthen Cover Letter Statements

Weak	Stronger
Improved productivity	Increased production by 20 percent over two years to 120 units per week
Increased efficiency	Reduced errors by 10 percent over first six months
Grew sales	Met sales goals consistently, increasing sales by 25 percent in first year to $400,000

Weak	Stronger
Reduced shrink	Reduced shrink by 15 percent, saving the firm $50,000
Managed a team	Managed team of six which met all sales goals within the first quarter
Reduced turnover	Developed program which reduced turnover by 15 percent
Consistently met goals	Exceeded sales goals by a minimum of 10 percent every cycle
Worked during college	Earned 50 percent ($25,000) of all college costs while going to school full time

Anywhere you can add quantification to your cover letter and résumé helps the hiring manager see your value. The saying goes: "If you can measure it, you can manage it," and that is what companies are looking for in their employees—*results*.

Table 12: Key Words to Use in Cover Letters and Résumés

Words to Avoid	Words to Use
• strong	• reduced
• exceptional	• improved
• good	• developed
• excellent	• researched
• outstanding	• created
• effective	• increased
• driven	• accomplished
• motivated	• won
• seasoned	• produced
• focused	• shaped
• dedicated	• achieved

Words to Avoid	Words to Use
• determined	• investigated
• eager	• gained
• persistent	• under budget
• zealous	• within plan/schedule

In table 12, you will note that the words to avoid are adjectives. This is because they describe a person's personality and not what they do. The list of words to use includes verbs—which therefore describe action, what a person does or can do—and the key to getting a job!

Statements of your accomplishments should speak to the items that are listed as required and desired skills for the position, and they should be verifiable; do not *fabricate* anything. Remember that your claims can be checked easily. Make sure that what you state is both accurate and meaningful for the position. It might not be relevant that you were a member of a social fraternity. However, if you stated that you were the president of the fraternity that could speak to your potential leadership abilities. If, in addition, you can add that during your presidency you grew membership by 10 percent, helped the fraternity increase their fundraising activities by 20 percent, or achieved other quantifiable accomplishments—you will strengthen your appeal to the hiring manager, assuming that these accomplishments fit the position requirements and preferred abilities.

If you know something about the company (specifics learned during your informational interviews—chapter 2, section 2), it might further support your application. Don't just reiterate something on their website, such as "Since xyz company is a leader in orphan drug research and I have always been interested in companies that are trail-blazers ..." This could appear to be a means of artificial aggrandizement and may turn off a prospective employer. However, if you stated that you knew that they were a company that was a leader in orphan drug research and that you had a cousin who benefited from xyz drug (not necessarily theirs but an orphan drug), this would be more truthful and possibly have impact. *If* you had a strong desire to make your career within a firm, finding out that the company you were interviewing with had a strong promotion from within policy would probably increase your interest. During your interview, you could state that you saw a fit with that policy and your interest in growing within a company. This might enhance your potential for an offer. However, without a firm base in actual behavior or in relationship to your interests, the statements could seem like just a way to puffery and ingratiating yourself.

The purpose of the cover letter is to influence the hiring manager / recruiter to read your résumé and then to set up an interview. Your cover letter is your ninety-second elevator speech to "hook" the fish. You will still need to get it into the boat (the interview) and finalize your catch before you can have lunch (the offer, negotiation, and hire). It should be brief but have impact. Cover letters are usually no longer than one page.

Section 4: The Closing and Follow Up

The closing should thank the reader for his or her consideration, state that you are looking forward to a personal interview, and state a time frame in which you will follow up. The time frame to follow up is usually between one and two weeks. However, this depends somewhat on the application deadline. For example, if you are applying on January 15th and the application deadline is February 25th, it is unlikely that the hiring manager will have much feedback (unless you are a definite *no*) before the middle to end of February.

Often cover letters end with a "thank you" and a "looking forward to hearing from you," but this leaves the applicant hanging and waiting for a call or letter—which might never come. Following up on a cover letter and résumé submission is important because you need to keep moving forward, and if you are waiting for a call that might never come, you are wasting time.

The worst thing that can happen when you follow up is that you are told that they will not be bringing you in for an interview or that they have hired someone else. At that time, you can ask for some feedback on anything you could have done differently to improve your application, which will help you in the future. Getting feedback—even just knowing this door was closed to you—can help you move on. Any feedback on your application means you have gained from the process. If you feel that the feedback is positive, you might even ask if there is anyone else that they would recommend you network with, either in their company or in another firm that might be of help.

Cover Letter Cautions

A word of caution and advice: most job ads seek "excellent communication skills," so it's important that your résumé and cover letter be perfect and devoid of any typos or grammatical errors. Most documents are written on Word, and if there is a green squiggly line under a phrase or sentence, it means that it has need of grammatical correction. If there is a red squiggly line under a word, it means that the word is spelled incorrectly. But remember that the computer is a machine (a great machine), so it cannot read your mind.

An example of an error that a student made (and wasn't caught by the grammar edits in Word) was the following: "It would be an honor for me to be apart of your organization." *Apart* as one word means the opposite of what the student was trying to convey. A second example of an error that I found in a cover letter: "After reading your advertisement on CareerBuilder I was excited to *cease* the opportunity in a growing company for which I am passionate." *Cease* means to stop, and the idea was to *seize*—or capture or grab—so this applicant was actually stating that they *didn't* want the opportunity.

If on your computer screen you see red or green, fix it before you print it or send it off to a prospective employer. Worse yet, if you submit it through the Internet, the red and green squiggles might show up to the reader of your application and be an instant signal to delete your application. Also, keep in mind that computer systems are not always perfect, as the "apart" and "cease" examples above did get through the Word screener without a green or red squiggly line. It's best to make sure that you have your submissions checked carefully, and an extra pair of eyes is always beneficial.

Section 5: Cover Letter Summary—Dos and Don'ts

Do

- personalize your salutation (make sure you have it correct— Mr., Ms., etc.),
- specify the job you are seeking,
- identify where you found the job listing,
- quantify your accomplishments and fit for the position,
- state that you will follow up (and when), and
- proofread.

Don't

- be too friendly in your opening,
- state that you have qualities without demonstrating them,
- restate the company's website claims (they know what they are),
- overstate your qualifications (puffery), or
- have any grammatical or spelling errors.

CHAPTER 6
RÉSUMÉS

- Avoid predictable, jargon-ridden formats typical of most résumés.
- Promote your keen understanding of current business issues.
- Go beyond past achievements, and convey your key quantifiable benefits.
- Write it as an exciting "proposal," not a dry summary of prior functions.
- Help employers see why you are potentially better than other candidates.

Employers want to know what they can expect if they hire you and are most pleased the more they can reduce their risk in hiring. Your résumé is your initial opportunity to reduce their feeling of uncertainty in their hiring decision, before they even have a chance to meet you.

I will begin with a pet peeve of mine, and that is the *objective*. Why do people put an objective on the top of their résumés? Most of the time, you can summarize your objective by stating: I want a job and perhaps more specifically, I want a job in your company doing the position that you posted in your advertisement. In this way, it is a waste of space and doesn't really help the hiring manager or you. It doesn't do anything to reduce their risk, and it reduces your chance of success!

Section 1: The Beginning

A better beginning can be a brief summary of who you are / what you can do / have done—for example, your elevator speech—or my personal recommendation is a list of your *key accomplishments.* That will provide you with a means to quickly show the hiring manager what you have done and help them to know what you can "bring to their party." A prospective employer is less interested in what you want than in what you can do for them and the company. Your key accomplishments will help them see if you are a fit based on what you have done in the past. Most people feel that a good predictor of future behavior is a look at past behavior. If you were an award-winning salesperson in the past, it is likely that you will meet your sales goals in a new company.

Like in your cover letter, numbers and quantification are important in your résumé, as they help to give dimension to what you have done. The examples below should give you an idea of some key accomplishments worded vaguely and dimensioned quantitatively.

Vague	Quantified
Consistently won corporate sales awards	Exceeded sales goals by 30 percent each year for the past five years
Worked full-time while going to college	Earned 80 percent of all university expenses
Met customer expectations and satisfied customers	Earned 90 percent top customer ratings
Received corporate recognition for customer service	Ranked in top three of all service providers (25) for two years
Graduated with a BA in business	Earned a GPA of 3.75 while attending university full-time and working a minimum of 35 hours per week

Vague	Quantified
Led my sales team in all categories; consistently exceeded quota	Top salesperson in four consecutive quarters; exceeded quota by 132 percent
Excellent leader and mentor	Maintained a 75 percent retention rate among team members; 35 percent of my team received promotions

Also, a listing of your key accomplishments can help you customize your résumé for each position to which you apply. It is probable that you have a limited number of key accomplishments; you should have at least three and probably no more than six listed. The order that you list them should be altered based on the position of focus. In this way, you can tailor your résumé, right from the beginning to the position of interest.

For example, if you seek a sales position, the accomplishment regarding sales would be listed first with your university/GPA accomplishment listed farther down in order. If you seek a customer service position, the accomplishment focused on customer service would move to the top position, and so on. You will need your own judgment based on the individual job ad and your experiences to determine the order of your accomplishments. If you feel that you have more than six key accomplishments, you can utilize them—choosing those most relevant to the current position for which you are applying.

Section 2: The Body

The next section of the résumé would either list your education or your work experience. This is determined based on both age and experience. If you are just graduating from college and looking for your first professional position—even though you have worked all through your educational journey—you would probably put your education first. If you worked during the pursuit of your degree in jobs relevant to the position you are seeking, then you could put your work experience first (before listing your education). For example, if you are applying for a store manager position and you worked in a similar retail setting while pursuing your degree, then putting your work experience first is an option. If you have always worked in retail as a sales clerk and you are completing your degree in finance trying to land a financial analyst position, you would probably put your degree first (BA in finance).

What you are trying to do with your résumé is to easily tell the most compelling story you can of your life/career journey to this point. You are interested in getting an interview (the next step) and landing a position that will move you to the next step on your career ladder. You do not want the reader to have to figure out the story.

Education Listing: Make sure that you list your degree(s) in reverse chronological order. (*Note:* There is no need to list your high school diploma, once you have at least an associate's degree.) When listing your education, include the name of your school, its location, your major area of study, any minor that you may also have earned, your GPA (and if higher, the GPA in your major), the year your degree was/will be granted (there is no need to put the beginning date also), and if supportive of your application, relevant course work. For example, if you are going for a human resources position with a financial services firm, you might list both your human-resources-related courses and finance courses under *relevant course work*. However, it would not be useful or necessary to list your accounting courses.

Listing your course work is a potential addition to the résumé, if you have space and *only* if it really helps to tell your story of your relevance/fit to the position.

Education
Rutgers University, School of Business, New Brunswick, NJ   May 2015
BS in business administration; major—management
GPA: 3.56

Key Course Work: human resources management, training and development, compensation management, financial management

---

Education
University of Michigan, Ann Arbor, Michigan   December 2015
BS in Biology
Major GPA: 3.40

Note: If you received your degree more than seven to ten years ago, the date of your graduation is less important, and your education section would probably go after your work experience. The "older" your degree is, usually, the less important the education detail is in terms of year of graduation, GPA, relevant course work, or awards.

Position Listing: List the jobs and internships that you have with the most recent/current position first and then going back in time. For each position, list the name of the company, the location, your job title, and the dates you worked there. Also, under each position, bullet point what you did and try to quantify your accomplishments and results here. The following table lists some examples of the ways you can quantify what your job entailed to make your résumé more compelling.

Basic Listings of efforts	Quantification of your efforts
Handled customer inquiries	Responded to an average of 200 customer inquiries a day with 90 percent high customer satisfaction ratings
Scanned customer purchases	Checked out an average of 40 customers per hour with consistent balanced cash draw
Sold cars to customers	Exceeded monthly sales quotas 60 percent of the time
Took customer deposits and cashed checks	Met customer needs for service while increasing balances and exceeding product acquisition quotas by 10 percent

---

Work Experience
Citibank, NA, New York, New York   6/2012–Present
Customer Service Manager
- Hired and trained 100 new CSRs
- Improved team's customer satisfaction ratings from 60 percent to 80 percent Very Satisfied
- Reduced team turnover from 70 percent to 10 percent during my tenure
- Developed a training protocol reducing training time by 20 percent

Gap Store, Montclair New Jersey,   8/2008–5/2012
Retail Store Associate, Assistant Manager
- Responded to 50 customers daily, meeting or exceeding weekly sales quotas
- Trained 10 new sales associates
- Led team of 5 in store management

JP Morgan Chase, New York, New York   6/2011–8/2011
Customer Service Summer Intern (part-time)
- Responded to 25 customer inquires daily with a 80 percent high satisfaction rating
- Learned banking systems for customer service

Note: You can include your internships within the work experience section or create a separate section, depending on how it supports your story and workflow. The cover letter of the above example would explain that the person worked in retail while in college for his or her BA in finance and one summer had an internship at a financial services company.

Section 3: Catch All—Skills / Certifications & Licenses / Awards / Volunteer Activities / Interests

The final section of your résumé (either after your position listings or education, whichever you decide would not go first after Key Accomplishments) would be the section that provides a place to lists skills, awards, any certifications or licenses, and interests/hobbies. Here is where you can add areas that don't fit within your other categories. This is a place where you can add color and depth to your personality and what you can do for the company.

Skills are things like languages (if you are bilingual or multilingual, list the languages you are fluent in), computer knowledge (and it is helpful to list the software specifically and what version of Microsoft office), and any technical knowledge that you have, whether or not it is relevant to the position. If you are facile in the use of Photoshop but it isn't part of the position, it still might be of interest to a prospective employer and it helps to complete a picture of you. Your abilities with social media would also go here, as that is a growing area of interest to businesses.

Certifications and licenses are areas where you may have earned a certificate or license that again will add to the picture of you. They can be job related (e.g., Series 7 License, Six Sigma black belt certification), or they can be in other areas (e.g., CPR certification, karate green belt). Often these can relate to your hobbies or outside areas of interest, and they help to paint a picture of you.

Awards are any specific awards that you have received. You should be a little circumspect about any awards that you mention, as you do not want to seem foolish. For example, if you were awarded the best costume in the most recent Halloween parade, that would probably not be something to list. However, if you were awarded a scholarship in school, received recognition for customer service, or were awarded

Employee of the Month at your place of work, these would be awards that support your application and should be added to the list.

Volunteer activities are those activities you do that you aren't paid for but where you give of yourself. If you ran a fundraiser for your organization or volunteered for Habitat of Humanity and built a home, these would show another side of you that might be impressive to a prospective employer. Again, any quantification here also strengthens the comment (i.e., how much you raised or number of homes worked on, etc.). However, if you only volunteered for four hours on one day, that might not warrant a place on your résumé. Always think about what something you put on your résumé says about you and whether or not it's something you wish a prospective employer to know. Will it help tell your story?

Interests are just that—how you spend your leisure time. They can provide an opportunity to display something about yourself that can make you stand out from the crowd or provide something for an interviewer or prospective manager to delve into and connect with. Are you a bassoonist, yoga enthusiast, or competitive bridge player? What do you spend time doing outside of work or classes? These areas can provide additional input for a hiring manager and might be of interest, even though they don't relate to the job.

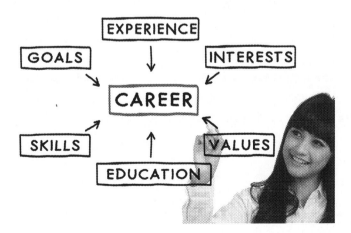

Skills/Certifications/Activities/Interests
- Microsoft Office: Excel, Word, PowerPoint, Access
- Photoshop, Adobe Acrobat
- Bilingual: English, Spanish
- CPR certification
- Volunteer emergency medical technician (Orange, SD 2009–present)
- Alpha Epsilon Delta member—national premed honor society
- Intermural soccer—University of South Dakota (2011–2015)
- Interests—travel, hiking, half marathons

Section 4: References (Not to Be Listed on Your Résumé)

There is no need to list references for a job on your résumé or even to write the phrase "references available on request" on your résumé. If they are required, you can provide the names and contact information at a later time. This is important because anytime you want to use references you should contact them in advance of their being called by the hiring manager.

References are typically asked for after an interview. That will give you the opportunity to check in with your references, make sure that they are available (and not on a two-week vacation out of the country or otherwise unavailable), and to give them some information about the position you are being considered for. In that way, they can tailor their recommendations to the company and position. Also, if your reference is someone who is used as a reference by several people, when the hiring manager calls, he or she will have had a heads-up and be prepared for the questions. It will make the reference call go more smoothly and be more successful for you.

Section 5: Format Considerations

Unless a résumé is for an academic or research position, it should not exceed a single page. Since academic résumés require a listing of multiple publications, they extend past the single page. Most hiring managers will get an abundance of résumés for any position, and they therefore usually spend less than two to three minutes reviewing résumés and cover letters. Recently I spoke to a manager who said that he received three hundred résumés for one administrative assistant position. Therefore, potential employers will discard an application (résumé and cover letter) that doesn't reflect accomplishments and address the key points that are of interest in a succinct way.

The top of your résumé should state your complete name and contact information, (mailing address, e-mail, phone numbers). Your résumé should be easy to read and businesslike. Your dates should be aligned either on the right hand or left hand side of your document so that a hiring manager can easily see your progression. Even though you should get your résumé on one page, you still need to make sure that it is clear and readable, so it's unadvisable to use exceedingly small type (less than 11 point) or squeeze spacing. Finally, unless you are in the arts or you are a model, you shouldn't use fancy fonts, colors, graphics, or include a picture on your résumé.

CHAPTER 7
INTERVIEWING

If you pass the hurdle of the cover letter and résumé and are called for an interview, then you have the opportunity to further your case to convince the employer to hire you. It is important that you prepare for this interview, whether it is in-person or on the phone. Either way, it is important for you to present yourself in the best possible way. This includes visual, verbal, and nonverbal means. When you are scheduled for an interview, being on time is critical. It sends the message that you feel this is a priority and that you know how to manage your time—two key messages to send to a prospective employer.

The main focus of this section will be in-person interviewing, as several of the areas relate to both in-person and on the phone. Preparing for any interview involves research of the company and position, so you can show that you are the right person for the position in terms of qualifications and fit with the company's culture. Being able to do the job is only part of what the interviewer will be looking for, as fitting in with the company culture will help ensure that you will be successful if hired.

Of course, when you go in for an interview, you must know where the interview will take place, how to get there (on time), and what to wear (the company look). In any interview, "fitting in" is a first step, and it begins with the first impression that the interviewer has of you.

> *Note:* An illustration to caution you about how you can sabotage your chances without realizing it is the following a story about an in-person meeting. The story is about a Harvard Medical School candidate who was taken to lunch by the admissions committee. During lunch he salted his hamburger before tasting it. After lunch with the admissions committee, his admission was denied. There are two versions of the rationale for their decision. They felt that he wasn't a good candidate because (1) he made a decision without relevant data (he didn't taste his hamburger before putting salt on it) or (2) he salted all his food (demonstrated by not tasting it first) and would develop heart disease early—and therefore would not be a good investment of the university's time in educating him, as he would die at a young age. This story is for illustrative purposes only and to caution you about how your in-person presence might be viewed by a potential employer.

Section 1: First Impressions

- Timing (Is Everything)
- Your Look (a Fit or Not?)
- Nonverbal Communication: Your Posture, Stance, Greeting
- What You Should Bring

Timing: The first thing is to make sure that you get to the interview on time; getting there fifteen minutes before the beginning of the interview is appropriate. If you do not know the exact location of the interview, it is good to take a dry run to ensure you can arrive on the date of the interview on time. Since unforeseen problems do occur—and if you find yourself stuck behind an accident on the road or some other catastrophe—make sure you have a cell phone and a contact number for the interview. If you find you will be delayed, contact the interviewer/company as soon as possible and state your apology and your situation. Ask if they will still have time to see you once you arrive. If not, try to reschedule during that contact.

Sometimes you might have to miss the interview due to unforeseen circumstances, and that situation could knock you out of the running for a position. If you aren't given another chance, it might be that they have many other candidates or that they are rigid. In either case, you might not have been a fit for them. At that point you should move on and consider it a learning experience.

Arriving too early (more than twenty minutes before the scheduled interview, unless you are told to arrive early to fill out paperwork or perform an assessment), doesn't necessarily demonstrate to the interview eagerness and something positive. It might make the office personnel uncomfortable and seem like you don't plan well. If you arrive very early for the interview, consider waiting outside of the office building in your car, or if in a city, find a local coffee shop and wait.

Your Look: In an in-person interview, your look is important. This might seem simple, but it is important. Knowing the company and their dress code will help you make a good impression. Here are some questions to ask yourself:

- For women: do they wear slacks, makeup?
- For men: do they wear suits, ties, or business casual; facial hair?
- For anyone: amount and type of jewelry, tattoos, piercings, hair length/design, shoes polished—nothing too ostentatious?

If you enter a company for an interview and you aren't dressed appropriately—you're either underdressed or overdressed—you could lose the opportunity for employment. It is easy to research what is appropriate in a number of ways: looking at the company's website will provide hints to its "corporate look," speaking to current employees, or even giving a call to human resources before the interview. Often new graduates make the error of underdressing, as they may not have an interview outfit—appropriate suit, tie, dress, sports jacket, pants suit, or business attire. However, sometimes being overdressed can also be a turnoff, as it shows you do not understand the company culture or position. Two examples of overdressing are below:

- wearing a suit and tie to a manual labor job interview where chinos and a collared shirt would be more appropriate
- wearing a high-end designer pantsuit and diamond jewelry for a position as a receptionist in a small walk-in health clinic, where a moderately-priced pantsuit and simple gold or costume jewelry would be more appropriate

Going to the restroom to check out your appearance before you go into your interview is a good idea. If you recently had breakfast or lunch, is there anything in your teeth or any crumbs on your face or clothes? Remember that you only have one opportunity to make a good first impression.

Nonverbal: In addition to what you wear, other nonverbal cues are important. How you enter the office and your carriage will give a clue to the interviewer about your level of comfort and assuredness. Stand up straight and have an assertive posture to let the interviewer know that you are comfortable and sure of yourself. Your entrance and greeting support the first impression that the employer has of you. Take your lead from the interviewer. Does he/she stand when you enter the room and offer his/her hand for a shake? If so, a firm, dry handshake is also an indication of your comfort with the situation. You also need to have strong eye contact. Looking at the interviewer directly shows strength, while avoiding eye contact sends a message of a lack of confidence. What you do with your hands during the interview can also be a plus or minus. You can use your hands to express yourself but not by waving them about. If you are nervous and your hands shake, you can leave them in your lap, but you should *not* sit on them.

What You Should Bring: You should bring a few things with you to the in-person interview: an extra copy or two of your résumé, a tablet and pen, and business cards (if you have them). When you begin the interview, you can ask if it is okay to take notes during your interview (having a tablet will be necessary). You don't have to take any notes, but it will allow you to jot down any items that you wish to follow up on, get back to, or to get additional clarification on at the end of the interview. If something comes up during the interview that you feel the need to clarify, your notes will remind you. You can then address it at the end of the interview or in your thank-you / follow-up note. Also remember to put away your cell phone after you turn it off!

The interview is your chance to show the hiring manager that you are a fit for the job and the company. The first impression you create should help you convince the interviewer that you are the best candidate for their opening. Research suggests that interviewers make up their minds in the first four minutes of the interview, and they spend the rest of the time trying to confirm their initial impression. Trained interviewers are asked to try to disconfirm their initial impression for accuracy, but either way, the first impression is important.

Section 2: Preparation

Researching the company and position beforehand is critical. Knowing the company, its industry, and what the position entails will provide you with the background you need to be more successful in the interview situation. It is often said that 80 percent of an interviewee's success is dependent on preparation.

Company website/talking to current employees: The organization's website will provide you with the company's focus, mission, and goals. Whether or not you are asked about your knowledge of their business concerns, you can garner points in an interview if you can show how you understand and can help support any of their business needs. In addition, during your informational interviews with current employees of the company, you can ask about their interviewing experience when they were being hired. If you are fortunate enough to know someone in the company, you can ask that person about his/her interviewing experience.

> I knew a candidate for an entry-level position at a financial services company who contacted a few of those who had been in the entry-level position for a year or two and interviewed them about both the job and what the interview process was like. He learned about what their problems were and key areas of need. Therefore, he was the most prepared for the interview. Even though his paper credentials would have placed him near the bottom of the list of candidates, he was the one selected.

If you can anticipate some of the questions that you will be asked, you will be better prepared for the interview. There are several ways to gather background information on the company and possible interview questions:

1. Searching the company's website
   a. Company vision, mission, credo
   b. Company financials, analyst reports, rating agency evaluations
   c. Customer reviews, testimonials
   d. What they are known for
   e. Current news items of interest
   f. Current activities and focus
   g. Any recent issues/problems
2. Talking to current employees
3. Checking out www.Glassdoor.com, or
4. Doing additional research on the company and/or interviewer (www.LinkedIn or Facebook.com might help here)

www.Glassdoor.com: This website's listings are by company. Its listings include ratings of companies by current and former employees. It also covers compensation and often includes interviewing questions that the candidates experienced. Since listings include company and position, you can gather insight into possible interviewing questions based on the company and—more broadly—based on the position. One of the additional benefits of Glassdoor is that individuals will more likely list a unique interview experience than one which is more standard, therefore broadening your perspective of the company and the potential interview.

Additional research on the company or interviewer: Learning more about the interviewer will be helpful for you to make a good impression and have a successful interview. Companies check out your social network presence, so you should check out theirs too. Can you find a Facebook or LinkedIn listing for the interviewer? If you have anything in common with the interviewer, that could be an opportunity for breaking the ice and getting over an uncomfortable beginning. When you cannot get any information before the interview, a cursory look around the person's office can provide some insight into them and their interests. Any additional knowledge of the interviewer can support your success.

Section 3: Overview of the Process—Q&A

You will be asked a lot of questions, and you should answer both thoughtfully and honestly. Thoughtfully means that you can take a few seconds before you answer to gather your response coherently and honestly. Do not embellish your accomplishments or claim unrealistic successes, as a good interviewer will uncover inconsistencies.

Interviewer questions: Most interviewers will begin asking questions based off your résumé and cover letter. They will ask to find out more in-depth about your stated accomplishments and what you have done in the past to determine how that fits with what they are looking for in an ideal candidate.

There are many common questions and areas that are used by most interviewers during the interview process. As a beginning, an interviewer will often ask the candidate the open-ended question: "Tell me about yourself." This is where your elevator speech comes in. An elevator speech is a forty-five to ninety-second autobiographical introduction. It comes from the idea that if you were to meet someone in an elevator, what would you say about yourself in the brief time before the door opened for your floor, to interest him or her in learning more about you. Of course, if you were thinking about the elevator speech that you would give to someone whom you just met at a bar or a party, it would be somewhat different.

When a prospective employer asks about you, it is your opportunity to engage them first thing so that the rest of the interview can be focused around your being an ideal candidate for the position. Your elevator speech will usually mention your education (if you are a recent graduate) and some of your experiences (relevant to the position of interest). It should also include some things that are somewhat unique about you that would be of interest to the interviewer. However, personal items or extraneous facts might not be of benefit. Being an archer or running marathons might be an interesting unique fact, but having multiple tattoos and piercings might not be.

Of course this takes both practice and knowing about the company and position beforehand (the reason for the informational interviews discussed in chapter 2). This is one question you can prepare for, as it is very often asked.

A second area of inquiry is often around you—and specifically your fit for the position. Below are a series of potential questions that could be asked:

- What do you see as your strengths?
- What do you most enjoy in your current position?

- What do you least enjoy in your current job?
- What are your weaknesses?
- What obstacles have you overcome?
- What are you most proud of? What is your biggest accomplishment so far?
- Why do you feel you are an ideal/good candidate for this job?
- Why should I hire you?
- Why do you want to work for this company?
- Why are you interested in leaving your current position?
- What would your current boss say about you if I asked?
- What leadership experiences have you had?
- What do you find the most challenging when working in a team?

Table 13 offers a list of potentially "scary" job interview questions that might put the interviewee on the defensive. You will need to be prepared for all types of questions, and how you answer the tough ones can set you apart from the crowd. You can turn the following questions into opportunities if you answer with forethought, honesty, and finesse. Although they might seem scary—as they are focused on the negative of someone's past experience—being prepared can make the difference between a failed interview and a job offer.

Table 13: Scary Job Interview Questions

What do you do poorly?
What are your weaknesses?
Tell me about a time when you failed.
Have you ever been fired or let go from a job?
Why did you leave your last job? (If you aren't currently working)
Why have you had so many short-term jobs or changed jobs so often?
Why do you want to leave your current job?
What was your role in your department's most recent failure?

In table 14, I have listed questions that I will call opportunity questions, as they have the ability to move you into the high-potential group of interviewees. Depending on your responses, the answers to these questions can set you apart from the average person being interviewed. Confidence, honesty, and forethought can provide you the chance to shine through the tough questions and show that you are a great candidate and someone that they should hire.

Table 14: Potential Opportunity Questions

Why should we hire you?
What would you hope to accomplish in your first ninety days here (or six months, year …)?
Give me an example of a problem you faced on the job and tell me how you handled it.
Provide some examples of how you've been able to motivate other people.
Tell me about a decision you made that was unpopular, and how you implemented it.
What was your role in your department's most recent success?
What can you do for us that someone else cannot?

Table 15 provides some answers to the opportunity questions that could help to make a difference in the outcome of your interview.

Table 15: Answers That Could Make a Difference

Questions	Guidance on Responses
Why should we hire you?	This question allows you to use your company research and focus your answer on what the company needs. What "points of pain" have you uncovered, and how can your education and experience help to address them? What would make you stand out and indicates that you are a "fit" for the position and the company in specific. How do you match the company culture?
What would you hope to accomplish in your first ninety days here (or six months, year …)?	Again, your research should guide you here as to their needs. What you can do that will help make the hiring manager feel he made the right decision? Are there short-term goals that you can meet? Longer-term ones?
Give me an example of a problem you faced on the job and tell me how you handled it.	Make sure that the problem you choose is relevant to the company you are interviewing for and the position you seek. Their "points of pain" should be your guide. Using an example with measurable outcomes and results will be the key to a great response. Make sure that you explain the problem, what you did to alleviate it, and the result in outcomes for the company. If this example and what you learned can be used in the company where you are interviewing, even better.

If you do not have an example from your actual experience, you can state how you would go about solving a problem that they are encountering (discovered in your research). Or if you have seen someone else do something and you learned from it, then that could be an example of your thinking and learning. Always make sure that you are focused on a quantifiable result, a measurable outcome, and a relevant issue that the company is facing. |

Questions	Guidance on Responses
Provide some examples of how you've been able to motivate other people.	This might be more difficult if you haven't had management or supervisory experience. However, you can use examples from other situations—with peers, classmates, or even relatives. The key is how you determined what was needed to get others to support what was necessary to accomplish the goals. Most of the time, motivating people is an individual process, as each person may have different wants or needs. Someone who realizes this has taken the first step in being able to motivate others and become a great manager.
Tell me about a decision you made that was unpopular and how you implemented it.	Again, this may be difficult if you haven't been in a supervisory or management position. However, it is similar to the above in that getting people to back your decision may be an individual process. You need them to see your viewpoint, and they may be coming from different points of view themselves. Any opportunity that you have had to show your ability to get something done with others (again, a group project for a class or a volunteer activity or club program) is a way to show capabilities that are needed in any company. Being able to move individuals to your point of view without bullying is a sought after skill in most companies.

Questions	Guidance on Responses
What was your role in your department's most recent success?	Here is a potentially dangerous question, as it can show your team skills or *not*. I once heard of an interviewee who stated that he didn't like the end project that his team put together for their assignment (a university class project), and he stayed up all night to "fix" it without consulting his group. They presented it to the professor. He stated that he was proud that they got an A, and he didn't tell the professor that he was the one who fixed it. The difficulty in this response was that he didn't demonstrate teamwork, even though that is what he thought he was conveying. Working with a group is a critical component of most jobs these days, and as the above questions tap, it is something that you should be able to demonstrate.
	Sometimes you do more than your share of work. However, if you take full credit for something that you were only partially responsible for, a smart interviewer can often uncover flaws and overstatements. This is also important in what you put in your résumé and cover letter, as you must be able to expand on those activities that you claim you did or participated in. Make sure here that you only take credit for what you were responsible for, and make it clear when you were a partner in the success.

Questions	Guidance on Responses
Or the reverse: What was your role in your department's most recent failure?	Caution here, as you do not want to blow off the question by saying, "We haven't had any failures" or stating that you have no responsibility. If you can think of something that didn't go totally perfectly—something that would show your humility and team effort without undermining your abilities or confidence—that would be useful. If you did have some responsibility in a recent failure, owning up to it and stating what you learned from the experience could put you right back in contention for the job. Employers are looking for people who can take responsibility and learn from their mistakes.
What can you do for us that someone else cannot?	Again, this should focus on what you have found their needs to be and how you are keenly able to support their needs through your talents. You can mention a particular success or how you would have answered one of the other questions listed above.

Overall, in responding to any question, you should be able to cite your accomplishments and successes in numbers and quantify how your efforts contributed to the outcomes and the company's results. This should be done in your cover letter, résumé, and when being interviewed. The strong word list in table 12 (page 42 and in appendix I) will also help you to do this.

Below are three additional ways to begin to respond to a broader range of questions by tailoring your response to advance your position in the interviewer's eyes:

1. "I have experience in exactly this area" (followed by specific examples)
2. "I'm a team player" (followed by stories of how you worked together with difficult team members)
3. "I'm proactive" (ideal talking point for start-ups and small companies)

It is best to be as prepared as possible before going into an interview, as it is your best chance to solidify your possible position with the company. To that end, I have included a list of additional questions in table 16 to provide an even broader range of possible areas of interviewer inquiry. This is to give you an opportunity to practice a wider range of responses.

Table 16: Additional Potential Interviewer Questions

a.	Give a time when you went above and beyond the requirements for a project.
b.	Who are our competitors?
c.	What was your biggest failure?
d.	What motivates you?
e.	What's your availability?
f.	Who's your mentor?
g.	Tell me about a time when you disagreed with your boss.
h.	How do you handle pressure?
i.	What is the name of our CEO?
j.	What are your career goals?
k.	What gets you up in the morning?
l.	What would your direct reports say about you? Your bosses? Your peers?
m.	What were your bosses' strengths/weaknesses?
n.	If I called your boss right now and asked him/her what area you could improve on, what would he/she say?
o.	Are you a leader or a follower?
p.	What was the last book you read for fun?
q.	What are your coworkers' pet peeves?
r.	What are your hobbies?
s.	What is your favorite website?
t.	What makes you uncomfortable?

u.	What are some of your leadership experiences?
v.	How would you fire someone?
w.	What do you like the most and least about working in this industry?
x.	Would you work forty-plus hours a week?
y.	What questions haven't I asked you?
z.	What questions do you have for me?

The final two questions listed above are important, because (1) they provide you a chance to make sure you have been able to give the interviewer the sense of you that you wish to portray, and (2) they allow you to gather additional information about the company, the job, and working for the specific manager. However, responding to the final question requires a word of caution. Not having any questions for the interviewer might make you seem uninterested or too surface. But by asking the wrong questions you could give the impression that you are only interested in what you will get from the job (e.g., just pay or time off) versus what you are bringing to the position. There is more about responding to question z below in the section Interviewee Questions.

If you want more targeted ideas of what may be asked at a specific company interview you can go to www.Glassdoor.com, as that site often has feedback from candidates who have interviewed at certain companies, and they post the questions that they were asked. This might also give you some additional ideas about what to expect in the interview.

Do not sweat: If you are prepared and you take your time, you can get through anything. Practice is the best way to be prepared for an interview, so role-play the interview process wherever you can. In addition, the more interviews you go on, the more relaxed you will be. Preparation also includes your research on the position and company (chapter 2, section 3).

No matter how much you prepare, there are times when interviewers will ask odd or curveball questions. Often these don't even seem related to the company or position, and they may be asked just to see the interviewee's reaction. In some instances, the interviewer does have a set answer that he/she is looking for, even though it may escape the regular person. If you are asked one of these odd questions, the only thing you can do is your best and try to respond.

My Experience with Curveball Questions

I remember many years ago, when I was in the process of applying for graduate school, I was asked what I felt was a strange interview question. I was asked, "What do you want written on your tombstone?" My answer was "I don't know, as I have never really thought about that." The interviewer didn't like my response and curtly said to me, "Well, everyone is going to die." Now that it has been many years later, I have often thought about what I could have said but still feel that my response was honest and adequate. Being true to yourself is important and should support a fit with the culture of the company.

In another interview, I was asked, "What type of artwork would you want to hang on the wall behind your desk?" The interviewer obviously didn't like my answer (I said something about animals), and when I asked him what my answer should have been, he said that I should have said a mirror, so that I could see who was behind me at all times if I had my back to the door. Although I didn't get that position, I felt that his response helped me to know that I wasn't a fit for the culture of that company, and not being offered the position was therefore fine with me.

Table 17 has a list of additional seemingly odd questions that various companies asked. Glassdoor gathers these questions annually and they can be found on their website at www.Glassdoor.com. Although these questions might not seem to make any sense to the regular interviewer or interviewee, they have been asked. That being said, my advice is to be calm and answer as best you can.

Table 17: Oddball Questions from Companies (found on Glassdoor.com and other sites)

If you were to get rid of one state in the United States, which would it be and why?" *(asked at Forrester)*
"How many cows are in Canada?" *(asked at Google)*
"How many quarters would you need to reach the height of the Empire State building?" *(asked at JetBlue)*
"What song best describes your work ethic?" *(asked at Dell)*
"Jeff Bezos walks into your office and says you can have a million dollars to launch your best entrepreneurial idea. What is it?" *(asked at Amazon)*
"What do you think about when you are alone in your car?" *(asked at Gallup)*
"Name 3 previous Nobel Prize Winners." *(asked at BenefitsCONNECT)*
If we came to your house for dinner, what would you prepare for us?" *(asked at Trader Joe's)*
"How would people communicate in a perfect world?" *(asked at Novell)*
"How do you make a tuna sandwich?" *(asked at Astron Consulting)*
"You are a head chef at a restaurant and your team has been selected to be on *Iron Chef*. How do you prepare your team for the competition, and how do you leverage the competition for your restaurant?" *(asked at Accenture)*
"My wife and I are going on vacation. Where would you recommend?" *(asked at PricewaterhouseCoopers)*
"Estimate how many windows are in New York." *(asked at Bain & Company)*
"What's your favorite song? Perform it for us now." *(asked at LivingSocial)*
"Calculate the angle of two clock pointers when time is 11:50." *(asked at Bank of America)*
"Have you ever stolen a pen from work?" *(asked at Jiffy Software)*
"Pick two celebrities to be your parents." *(asked at Urban Outfitters)*

"What kitchen utensil would you be?" *(asked at Bandwidth.com)*
"If you had turned your cell phone to silent, and it rang really loudly despite it being on silent, what would you tell me?" *(asked at Kimberly-Clark)*
"If you could be anyone else, who would it be?" *(asked at Salesforce.com)*
"How would you direct someone else on how to cook an omelet?" *(asked at PETCO)*
And one of my favorites from my students: If you were a bicycle, what part would you be, and why?

Although unusual questions can throw you off balance, candidates should be ready to take on challenging questions. The strange questions can torpedo an interview if you let them. Take a breath and answer as best as you can. If you don't have an answer, you can state that too. If you feel it is important, you can note it down and perhaps provide a response in your thank-you letter

Interviewee questions: An interviewer almost always ends the interview with the following question: "Do you have any questions for me?" This is an opportunity to find out about the manager, the job, and the company. Table 18 covers questions that both show the interviewer that you are the right candidate and help you determine if this is the right position and company for you.

Table 18: Interviewee Questions That Can Make a Difference

Potential Good Questions and what they can demonstrate

A. Demonstrating Interest	
What would I have to do in the next 30, 60, 120 days to make you feel that you made the right decision in hiring me?	Any of these questions would demonstrate your interest in pleasing the manager by knowing what is important to him or her in who is hired. In addition, the answer would give you additional insight into the position and the manager that could help you make a decision, if you were offered a job.
What would make the person in this position a superstar?	
What are the biggest unmet needs in your department currently?	
What could the ideal candidate do to make your job easier?	
What areas could I focus on to really make a difference?	
What do you like best about working for this company?	This demonstrates interest and will provide you insight into the company culture and the manager's personality.

B. Establishing Expectations and Showing Drive	
What would you say are the three most important skills required for this position?	This will tell you about what they are expecting from you and help you decide your fit. Often a manager's answers are personality or work-style based, and you will be able to identify quickly if you feel you are a good match.

B. Establishing Expectations and Showing Drive	
How is success in this department measured?	These questions demonstrate your desire to succeed, perform well, and your interest in a career with the company and not just a job.
What is the progression plan for this position?	

C. Assessing the Manager's Style	
What are you most proud of that you have done in the past year?	Asking this of a manager will help you to know if he/she is more focused on the team or themselves and will provide you with information about fit with the manager.

D. If you feel that the interview was going well, you might continue with these questions to assess where you stand in the interviewer's perception	
Do you feel my skills and experience align with what you are looking for?	If asked in a friendly inquisitive way, this can help you appear self-confident and it can open the door for honest feedback. You may also then share additional information beyond your résumé that shows you are an ideal candidate for the job.
Based on our conversation and my application, could you tell me of any doubts that you have about my ability to succeed in this position?	This might give you another chance to demonstrate your fit and show the interviewer of your continued interest.
What are the next steps in the process? Do you have a decision deadline? What is it?	This will provide you with information about where you stand, help you with planning, and let them know of your continued interest.

When the interviewer asks if you have any questions, it is usually not a good response to state that you do not have any. This often suggests a lack of interest, poor listening skills, or that you are not really engaged in the interviewing process. Table 18 has a list of questions that can be used in most any interview in response to an interviewer's open-ended question. Of course, you can ask other questions about items that may have come up during the interview.

Remember that you are not yet in a strong negotiating position, and you do not want to send the wrong message to the hiring manager. Therefore you do not want to ask certain questions (even though you might be interested in the answers), as some questions will send a warning flag to the interviewer. Some examples of questions *not* to ask as a response to the interviewer's end question are:

Poor Questions

What does this job pay?
How long before I get a promotion/raise?
What benefits do you offer?
How long do I have to work before I get a paid vacation?
Can I work from home?
How much sick time do we get?
What are our hours? When do I have to be here in the morning?

The above questions only demonstrate your interest in what you will get out of working for the company and not what you feel you can bring to the company. Although the job interview is somewhat of a negotiation, before you are made an offer, the balance of power is with the interviewer. You do not want to add to that by asking questions only about what they will be offering.

Section 4: Next Steps—Follow Up

After your interview, make sure that you send a note of thanks to all those with whom you spoke. Most often you will be given business cards that have e-mail addresses on them, and you should use them so that you can follow up right after the interview. Your thank-you notes should be sent within twenty-four to forty-eight hours after the interview, and they are another opportunity to make a good impression. If a question arose during your interview and you were not satisfied with your answer, you have a chance to follow up on it in your thank-you note. It is also a time to reinforce your interest in the position and company. A quick thank-you allows you to stay upfront in the interviewer's mind.

If there was discussion of timing of the decision, you can also add something about your follow up to the note. This shows interest and continues to support your desire for the position.

Finally, if you are no longer interested in the position, you can state that in a thank-you note with an explanation of why your interest changed. Make sure that your reason for change does not put you in a bad light (e.g., I didn't realize we worked long hours and weren't paid for overtime), but rather is a reason that could keep the door open for other opportunities within the company if you are still interested in working in that environment. An example of this would be stating that you didn't realize that this position would require relocation after six months, and due to your spouse's employment, relocation this soon would not be possible. This would leave a good impression with the interviewer, increasing your networking and keeping potential doors open for future opportunities.

CHAPTER 8
THE OFFER AND POTENTIAL NEGOTIATION

Now the fun part begins. At some point in your process of job searching, cover letter / résumé writing and interviewing, you will be made a job offer. If it is a position that you want, feel that you are a match for, and the offer is what you feel is sufficient, then the answer may be an easy yes.

However, if you are not sure that you understand the job offer or the expectations, it is best to make sure that you have everything clarified before accepting the offer. Sometimes the offer letter does not state some of the information and agreements that you discussed with the manager, and those could be areas in need of clarification.

Example: If the manager mentioned that performance reviews occurred on a twelve-month cycle, and you felt that your discussion with the manager led to an agreement of an initial performance review in six months, that would be something that you would want clarified and probably in writing.

Companies will usually put an offer in writing, and you should be comfortable with the terms of the offer. This is usually less complicated when you are early in your career or starting your first job. Later in your career, when you are leaving a company, you will need to be aware of anything you may be giving up when you leave and how the new company compares to what you are walking away from (e.g., stock options, nonvested pension monies, etc.).

Most companies are somewhat clear in the offer letter. If there are questions regarding benefits, those can usually be addressed to human resources prior to accepting a position. If any special or out of the ordinary issues or agreements came up during the interview process, make sure that you have written confirmation so that questions or problems do not arise after you begin working (note previous **Example**). These can be things such as specific working hours, time off for a preplanned vacation (prior to earning vacation days), working from home, accelerated promotion reviews, etc.

Sponsorship Agreements/Offers: If you need sponsorship, that's an area that you will also have to negotiate. You need to ensure that any sponsorship agreement is clear from both sides. Make sure of your understanding of what the company will do for you, and they will need to make sure they know what you need from them. This is something that usually is in the purview of human resources, and the hiring manager may need assistance within the company to finalize the process. Since the laws vary depending on the type of sponsorship needed, it is necessary to work closely with the company to make sure everything is correct.

Usually benefits are standard in a company, and if there is a choice, it is the same for everyone in a certain role. Start dates can be negotiated, and a planned vacation that falls before vacation time is earned usually can be negotiated as time off without pay.

However, salary is often a negotiated item, and getting the compensation you seek happens before you begin working. After you start, there is little room to negotiate for greater salary, prior to a performance review or promotion.

If the position has a range of pay and you are offered a salary at the lower end of the range, there might be some room to negotiate for a higher starting salary. This would be based on what you are bringing to the company in terms of experience, skill, education, or expertise. If you aren't offered the salary you seek but are interested in the position, you can try to negotiate for an earlier (than one year) review of your performance for an increase in your compensation. Depending on the company, this may not be possible, as many larger companies are quite rigid in their policies.

One other possibility for additional compensation would be dependent on how you found the position/company. If you found the position on the company website, there is probably little room for negotiation. However, if it was a position listed with a search firm (often more senior positions)—but you didn't go through the search firm as you were a referral from another worker, and the hiring manager did not have to pay a search firm's fee—then perhaps a signing bonus could be obtained, as they saved the fee. This would only be likely if the search fee was not paid.

In any negotiation, you must be clear on what you want, what you are willing to give up, and if you are willing to actually walk away. If you are not clear on what you must have and you aren't willing to give up the position, you are not in a negotiating position.

If you are just starting your career, relax. Although you might not get everything you want, remember that this is just the first step on your career ladder. Most individuals starting careers now will work in at least seven or eight different organizations before they retire, and this could mean at least twice as many different positions.

ENDNOTES

As an endnote: When I worked full time as a consultant to many large companies involved in assessing their employees' satisfaction or engagement, I was asked why there were so many questions on the survey my company administered to measure employee satisfaction. Our clients asked if there was one question that could really tap into a person's connection to his or her job, and I came up with one.

If you won a significant amount of money (say $5–10 million after taxes), would you be at your current position in a month?

I tested the question on those whom I felt were engaged in their positions and those who weren't, and the answers I got supported that this was a good surrogate question for assessing the attachment people have to their jobs. The amount of money had to be enough to make money not a driving force for the work, and the month was enough time for someone to feel that they had freedom but would miss what they enjoyed doing. That is my hope for all—that you find fulfilling work. I want you to find a position that is a good match for your strengths, interests, and talents and with a company that is also a culture fit so that you can "eat for a lifetime"—content.

APPENDIX A
PERSONAL ASSESSMENTS

In my class, I have students take the Career Occupational Preference System assessment (COPS), made up of 192 items for which students note their level of interest. The inventory is then scored to provide individuals with feedback on both where their interests lie and how that could translate into a possible job/career area. Even for upper level college students (who have already declared their major), college graduates, and people who have already begun their careers, an interest inventory can be a means of verifying their choices or helping to redirect their job search activities.

There are many assessments that tap into one's work styles and interests. Two of the most common and widely used are the Myers Briggs Type Indicator (MBTI) (http://www. humanmetrics.com/) and the Strong Interest Inventory. Some are free and can be found on the Internet, while others have fees associated with them. They should all be taken as support to your career direction and not absolutes, and they shouldn't force you to change direction if that is uncomfortable to you.

Be aware that there are no right or wrong answers in these assessments. Knowing the results can help you understand where you might best find comfort, and possibly pleasure, in a job. It is understandable that a person who is high on the extravert dimension might not be happy in a nine to five data analysis job, chained to a desk, with little or no interactions with others during the day. Also someone who "hates people" will not be happy doing a receptionist's job.

If you choose to take one of these assessments, it is important to take it honestly and to answer as you really feel rather than how you think you should respond. The responses are often a mix of confirmation and some surprises. Consider all the findings, and see if the surprises can help you to broaden your view of possibilities.

You can discuss your findings with a friend, teacher, relative, significant other, or career counselor to get additional feedback.

You can access the free inventory on the site and can take several free online assessments. Remember, however, that you often get what you pay for; these should therefore be taken as a guideline and not an absolute. Any information that you gather during your career journey should be considered as input and help you along the way. Remember, there is no firm road map for this journey, as there are often bumps on the road. Some are helpful (possible shortcuts), while others may detour you and make your journey more tedious.

It will be helpful to gather additional information on any career area that you uncover during your interest inventory exploration. This is a good time to go back to the informational interview step to find out more about that position/career area.

The Myers Briggs Type Indicator has a number of questions/items and results in designations of one of two levels of each of four personality types that result in sixteen possible combinations. It measures introversion/extroversion, sensing/intuition, thinking/feeling, and judging/perceiving. This assessment can be taken for a fee at the previous listed site (page 91).

HumanMetrics offers a free personality assessment at the site: http://www.humanmetrics.com/cgi-win/jtypes2.asp. This is similar to the Myers Briggs assessment. If you take this assessment it will result in a four-letter type description of your personality type, as does the Myers Briggs assessment. It also provides a description of your preferences that can help you in determining your career and occupational direction.

The Strong Interest Inventory measures your interests in a range of occupations based on work activities, leisure activities, and school subjects that are applicable to a variety of work choices.

Additional alternative to Myers Briggs and Strong Interest Inventory Assessments:

- CareerNoodle—http://www.careernoodle.com
  Under Advice & Assessment, choose either My Interests or My Values. CareerNoodle provides a suite of engaging, authoritative, and easy-to-use exploration and planning tools for middle, high school, and college students. Utilizing active and constructivist learning theories combined with advanced web technologies, CareerNoodle was created with a user-centered design process that included the participation of hundreds of guidance counselors, educators, and students across the nation.

- CareerOneStop—http://www.careeronestop.org
  Choose Explore Careers. Choose Find Assessments under Self-Assessments. CareerOneStop is your pathway to career success, featuring the broadest and deepest collection of information about careers on the web. CareerOneStop has information and tools to help job seekers, students, businesses, and career professionals.

- My Next Move—http://www.mynextmove.org/explore/ip
  The O*Net Interest Profiler can help you find out what your interests are and how they relate to the world of work. It can assist you in deciding what kinds of careers you might want to explore.

There is a tremendous amount of information, assessments, and guidance on the Internet about various careers. I have done some initial searches and provided several sites and links to get you started. These should be taken as starting points as you initiate your career journey. Do not be afraid to venture into great depth into any of these assessments—as the more you learn about yourself, the better the fit with your work and the more engaged you will be.

The site: www.career-descriptions-and-jobs.com provides a lot of career and job information. If you go to www.about.com and type in Free Career Tests and Career Aptitude Tests or to www.livecareer.com, you will find many additional free career interest tests. These can provide input into understanding your areas of interest and resulting long-term job engagement. Think about when you were in school; the classes that you most enjoyed and did well in were the ones that most held your interest.

Additional free interest assessments can be found at:

- Holland Code Career Test: http://www.truity.com/test/holland-code-career-test
- O*Net Interest Profiler: http://www.mynextmove.org/explore/ip
- ISEEK's Career Cluster Interest Survey: https://www.iseek.org/careers/clusterSurvey
- www.free-career-test.com
- www.assessment.com

Finally, below is a list of various assessments with brief descriptions that can help you better understand your interests and personality and provide some insight to inform your job search:

Color Career Test

ColorQuiz is a quick and easy five-minute test that analyzes your personality based on the colors you select.

Dewey Color System Test

The Dewey Color System is a color-based career test that can give you information on jobs that would be a good fit. You simply click on the colors you like and the colors you don't like to get a list of suggested occupations.

Is This the Right Career for You?

Which career is right for you? Take a career quiz, or two, or three. Find out which career is suitable for someone with your personal characteristics.

Jung Typology Test

Click to select an answer to seventy yes or no questions. This will provide you a personality type formula according to Carl Jung and Isabel Briggs Myers typology, along with the strengths of the preferences, a description of your personality type, and a list of occupations that are most suitable for you.

Keirsey Temperament Sorter

The Keirsey Temperament Sorter, another top rated test, helps you discover what type of temperament you have and tells you if you're an Artisan, Guardian, Rational, or Idealist (free description with an option to purchase the full report).

Monster Career Tools

Monster's Career Management tools let you research occupations using Career Snapshots, compare yourself to others using Career Benchmarking, and explore career paths using Career Mapping.

Sokanu

Sokanu is a free platform for users to assess their interests, personality type, abilities, values, and preferred work and social environments in order to find matches that will lead to satisfying careers. Sokanu suggests careers after users respond to a series of questions. Detailed information is available on each of the suggested career options.

More Career Tests

More assessments are available, including free career tests, personality tests, career aptitude tests, career quizzes, and career assessment tests.

APPENDIX B
STRENGTHS ASSESSMENT

The Gallup Organization developed the Clifton StrengthsFinder and led the way in providing employers and employees with a way to view the fit of a person to a position. The Clifton StrengthsFinder consists of 180 paired statements of activities from which you are asked to choose your preference. The assessment uses a scale that evaluates the degree of the preference. The outcome provides an assessment of a person's leading themes and the way in which a person handles his or her environment. The thirty-four strengths of the assessment cover Relating, Impacting, Striving, and Thinking Themes. After learning what your leading strengths are, they advise that you focus on what you do best and manage around your nonstrengths. You can get a code to take a Clifton StrengthsFinder by purchasing one of the books. The resulting output of the assessment through the book code is a list of your top five strengths. My experience is that it is important to know not only your top five strengths but also your bottom five (as that will help you to know what you should be "managing around").

Other organizations have developed strength assessments that can be accessed for free on the Internet. The one I mention in the front of the book is http://freestrengthstest.workuno.com/free-strengths-test. html. This site consists of a number of activities for which you rate your interest. With the free assessment, you receive a complete list of all thirty-four strengths in order; however, it is possible that the differential between several is either very small or nonexistent. In this way, you might not get a clear top five and bottom five. Because you are not forced to choose between two items, the results can end up in inflated scores on many items and resulting strengths numbers. Since this is not a paired comparison (i.e., a forced choice between two items) but a simple rating, the results are not as discriminating as those of the Clifton StrengthsFinder, which uses a paired comparison. The results of the Clifton StrengthsFinder clearly lists the top five, and if the complete assessment is purchased, it provides an ordered listing of all thirty-four strengths—without any overlap of strengths ratings.

- The free site provides details around the meaning and leanings of the strengths. It also has additional information and direction on how to use your findings.

APPENDIX C

USING YOUR STRENGTHS ASSESSMENT

Once you have completed your strengths assessment, it is helpful to ask yourself some questions to delve into your results and use what you discover.

1. What strengths are at the top of your results? What were at the bottom? Were they what you expected? Did anything surprise you?

   _____

   _____

   _____

   _____

2. How have you seen your strengths play a role in your life—both personally and at work? How have the nonstrengths impacted you?

_____

_____

_____

_____

3. If you could do any job, what would it be? What makes it appealing? How do you think it fits with your strengths?

_____

_____

_____

_____

4. Are you prepared to do that job right now? If yes, is there anything holding you back? If no, what is holding you back? How do your strengths or nonstrengths help or hinder your preparedness?

_____

_____

_____

_____

5. Do you have a view of where you would like to be in three to five years? What steps do you think will help you get there? What opportunities would support your journey? What might be obstacles? How can you use your strengths to assist in this effort?

_____

_____

_____

_____

6. Of the positions you have held, what has been the most rewarding? What has been the most disappointing? If you view these from your own strengths perspective, can you learn anything that will help you in the future?

_____

_____

_____

_____

APPENDIX D
ADDITIONAL COPS INFORMATION

The Career Occupational Preference System (COPs) helps you define the kind of work you would be most interested in and can point you in a direction for type of position.

The COPS assessment provides you with a direction of what kind of work you will most enjoy. Ideally, a person would take such an interest inventory while in high school or before selecting a final major in college, but that doesn't always happen. Taking an interest assessment will help you to put an entire picture of yourself together, so that you can better focus your job search activities. Sometimes this is helpful for people who are becoming disillusioned or dissatisfied with their current career and seek a change. If you have access to a COPS or other interest assessment tool through work or school, it is advisable to avail yourself of one or more of these tools. These assessments usually cover a wide range of possible interests and may help one uncover areas that haven't been previously considered.

I have access to the COPs assessment for my classes, and I use this to help students better identify their areas of interest. This assessment is something that can be done in high school, early in one's college career, or whenever you want to see where your interests lie. The COPS Interest Inventory consists of 192 items, providing job activity interest scores related to the fourteen COPS System Career Clusters.

The COPS inventory results in a profile comparing your results to those in the designated fields assessed. Each cluster is keyed to an educational curriculum, as well as current sources of occupational information. You can find additional information on this assessment at http://www.edits.net/support/technical-support/copsystem-3c-faqs.html.

To give you some idea of the categories of interest covered in these assessments, I have listed the sixteen areas that COPS covers:

• science—medical life	• business—finance
• science—physical	• business—management
• technology—electrical	• communication—written
• technology—mechanical	• communication—oral
• technology—civil	• arts—performing
• outdoor—nature	• arts—design
• outdoor—agribusiness	• service—instructional
• computation	• service—social

Examples of Possible Jobs Based on COPS Interest Areas:

Science	medical—botanist, audiologist, food scientist, oral surgeon, pathologist, pharmacist, surgeon ...	physical science—chemistry, oceanography, meteorology, perfumer, soil scientist ...
Technology	engineer—mechanical, electrical, safety, nuclear ...	designer—network, software, manufacturing ...
Outdoor	nature—conservation, fish and game, forester, landscaper, miner ...	agribusiness—animal scientist, animal trainer, beekeeper, farmer, breeder ...

Business	finance—accountant, banking, programmer, economist, estate planner ...	management—customer service, program mgr. director, store mgr., hospital administrator ...
Computation	actuary, database administrator, records management ...	financial analyst, logistics engineer, programmer, statistician, price analyst ...
Communication	written—editor, librarian, author, historian, copywriter ...	oral—announcer, dispatcher, lawyer, lecturer, teacher ...
Arts	entertainment—director: music, sports, stage; musician, choreographer, model ...	fine arts—architect, costumer, curator, fashion design, jeweler, landscape architect, painter, sculptor ...
Service	instructional—teacher, coach, guidance counselor, occupational therapist, educational director ...	health—nurse, psychologist, therapist, fire inspector, community relations advisor, investigator, funeral director ...

APPENDIX E

BEGINNING QUESTIONS FOR INFORMATIONAL INTERVIEWS— POSITION FOCUSED

- What does a typical day look like in this position?
- What do you like most about this job?
- What do you like least about this job?
- What most surprises you about this position?
- What would you like to change about this position?
- What background—education and experience—did you need to get this position?
- What did you do right before you began this job?
- What do you wish you had known before taking this job that you know now?
- What do you wish you could do more of at this job?
- What do you wish there was less of at this job?
- If you had to do it over again, what other classes and/or work experiences would you have taken/gotten before starting this job?
- If you could have any job, what would it be, and why (if not this one)?
- Add your own:
- _____
- _____
- _____

APPENDIX F

QUESTIONS THAT DEFINE COMPANY/WORK ENVIRONMENTS

- What do you like most about working for this company?
- What do you dislike most about working for this company?
- Do you feel recognized for your accomplishments at this firm?
- How would you rate the management at the company?
- Do you feel that there is opportunity for advancement at this company? If yes, what does it take to advance?
- Would you state that this company is focused on production or people or both? Why?
- What has been your biggest surprise since joining this company?
- If you could change anything about this company, what would it be?
- Is there anything that you hope never changes about the company?
- If you could work for any company, which one would you choose and why?
- Add your own:
- _____
- _____
- _____

APPENDIX G
JOB SITES — USING THE INTERNET

You can find numerous sites that will aggregate the potential positions available. If you enter various key word or phrases to search on the web, many different sites will be listed. Below are a few key phrases:

- job listings, job sites, job search engines
- career opportunities
- position openings, position search engines
- internships

Below is a list of additional job sites that are used by many. Since there are constant changes and additions to what is available through the Internet, I suggest you add your own search findings to the list. Your interests, type of position desired, and experience might provide useful additional key words and direction for your search.

www.altavista.com	jobs/search engine
www.americanjobfairs.com	job fairs
www.anywho.com	online directory
www.computerwork.com	computer jobs
www.hotbot.lycos.com	jobs/search engine
www.jobs.com	jobs/search engine

www.jobs.net	jobs/search engine
www.mamma.com	jobs/search engine
www.net-temps.com	technical jobs
www.nytimes.com	*NY Times* ads
www.search.computerjobs.com	computer jobs
www.yahoo.com	jobs/search engine
www.6figurejobs.com J	jobs/search engine
www.about.com	jobs/search engine
www.allretailjobs.com	retail jobs
www.brassring.com	IT, sales, and HR
www.careerjournal.com	*Wall Street Journal*
www.employercontact.com	company listings
www.execsearches.com	education and nonprofit
www.federaljobs.net/index.html	federal jobs
www.flipdog.com	jobs/search engine
www.glocap.com	it/fin/legal/management jobs
www.hcareers.com	hospitality/health
www.higheredjobs.com	jobs/search engine

APPENDIX H
LIST OF WEBSITES FOR ADDITIONAL INFORMATION

- www.6figurejobs.com—job search site for positions over $100,000
- www.beyond.com—a career network for job seekers
- www.Careerbuilder.com—a job site where positions can be e-mailed to you
- www.CareerJimmy.com—tools to find jobs
- www.careerprofiles.com—career and job search database
- www.Careers.org—a guide to career resources and positions
- www.Execunet.com—a community for job seekers
- www.experteer.com—jobs for executives over $100,000
- www.Gallup.com—additional information about Strengths information
- www.Glassdoor.com—reviews of jobs and companies, including salaries and benefits
- www.Ivyex.com—career resources for executives
- www.LinkedIn.com—manage your professional identity, network, and get career advice
- www.profilesinternational.com—a consulting firm that helps companies assess candidates and provides guidance that helps job seekers

- www.RipoffReport—reviews of companies from current and past employees, scams
- www.Thecareernews.com—a weekly newsletter regarding careers and job searching
- www.Theladders.com—a personalized job search site
- www.themuse.com—career advice

APPENDIX I
KEY WORDS TO USE AND AVOID

Words to Avoid	Words to Use
• strong	• reduced
• exceptional	• improved
• good	• developed
• excellent	• researched
• outstanding	• created
• effective	• increased
• driven	• accomplished
• motivated	• won
• seasoned	• produced
• focused	• shaped
• dedicated	• achieved
• determined	• investigated
• eager	• gained
• persistent	• under budget
• zealous	• within plan/schedule

BIOGRAPHY

Dr. Chlopak, a PhD industrial/organizational psychologist from Ohio State University, has more than thirty years of experience as an educator, entrepreneur, consultant, and manager working with the largest corporations in the world, including Citibank, AT&T, and the Gallup Organization. She has also taught both graduate (MBA) and undergraduate business  students at Rutgers, Stevens Institute of Technology, Baruch College (CUNY), Montclair State, Seton Hall, and Kean. These have provided her with important insights and experiences in the conduct of today's labor market. These insights are the foundation of what is necessary to compete and land successful jobs today, leading to rewarding careers.

Since the economic downturn in 2009, she has worked with numerous adults in their quest to find suitable starting positions or in redefining themselves to land their next professional job. Her passion is helping individuals to identify, find, and secure placements that are engaging and supportive of career goals.

She and her husband of forty-two years live in New Jersey and have succeeded in raising three professional daughters and now also enjoy two granddaughters. Dr. Chlopak and her husband are each continuing in their business careers while they mentor and provide guidance to students and colleagues in their career efforts.

Printed in the United States
By Bookmasters